JUST FOR THE FAMILY

DAVID LUBBOCK

authorHOUSE®

AuthorHouse™
1663 Liberty Drive
Bloomington, IN 47403
www.authorhouse.com
Phone: 1 (800) 839-8640

Published by AuthorHouse 04/09/2015

ISBN: 978-1-4969-7358-0 (sc)
ISBN: 978-1-4969-7359-7 (hc)
ISBN: 978-1-4969-7357-3 (e)

Print information available on the last page.

ACKNOWLEDGEMENTS

David Miles Lubbock (DML), "Big D" in my family, wrote and dictated this memoir, *Just for the Family*, in the summer of 1992. Thanks to Jean James who transcribed DML's dictation and handwritten notes. Thanks also to her husband Professor Philip James who was Director of the Rowett Research Institute at this time. Professor James's interest in DML's knowledge gave DML added sense of purpose: he believed that the fight for a better world through food and nutrition would be carried on and that he himself could continue to contribute. Thanks to Lois McNaughton and Roisin Maguire for additional manuscript work as it was edited and re-ordered. Thanks to Moira Lubbock for editorial work.

In his last written communication to me he wrote that he was leaving the book for me to finish. "Note from Big D: I am afraid I have made absolutely no progress with the book… I will write you for the record, to thank you for your help and ask you to finish it and for it to belong to you.

All our love. Waterbed dry last night. Here's hoping!

Au revoir somewhere sometime somehow."

Sorry for the delay. I hope it has matured like a good Bordeaux.

KMBL
March 2015

CONTENTS

David Miles Lubbock

1911-1992

PROLOGUE

Brother Peter and I came at the end of a long concatenation. (The lineage can be seen from the family trees, which I adored.) We were born at Broadoaks, Byfleet, Surrey, he in 1909 and I in 1911.

Our mother, née Miles, had previously been married to Sir Charles Tennant, Bart of the Glen, Innerleithen in the Borders. He had had 12 children by his first wife, née Winsloe, and when she died he married our mother and they had four daughters. One died as a young girl. The youngest, Nancy, was born when "The Bart", as he was commonly called, was 81 years old. He was born in 1823 and died in 1906 aged 83. Three years later our mother married our father, Geoffrey Lubbock, and they had just us two. As I weighed 12 1/2lbs when I was born and took three days to arrive, it is not surprising that my poor mother did not have any more.

Peter and I, although not descended from Tennant genes, nonetheless have been environmentally strongly affected by Tennants especially our three half-sisters. It has been said by friends that while one Tennant at a time was fun, more than one was unbearable! We had three living in the family with our parents. They, like many children with a step parent, did not like our father. This created a strain which I believe aggravated Peter's asthma which originated at birth as eczema. His poor health and my good health resulted in our gradual space separation though we were always fond of each other and the sisters were kind and generous to us both. In the next generation Sister K, who had no children, treated my four children as her own.

Our mother, who was the linchpin of the concatenation, came from the West Country (Gloucestershire) Miles family. They were probably slave-traders who rose to prominence in Bristol and eventually owned the Avon docks. Whether they had any connection with Brunel or not

I don't know. But I would not be surprised if they had, because of the benefit they would have received if his magnificent scheme of transport communication between the Americas through Bristol and London to Europe had succeeded. Brunel does come into the family picture however in that Jan Gooch's forefather, Daniel Gooch, was Brunel's engineer.

Our mother's parents and family were yeomen, keen on hunting (with the Beaufort) and military (Uncle Napier was Colonel of "The Blues," the crack Royal Horse Guards). Mummy was a violinist and once played lead in a symphony under the baton of Sir Hamilton Harty, an outstanding conductor. Her mother, née Hill, was an artist, she drew beautiful pen and ink sketches on the envelopes of her letters.

The Tennants were from south-west Scotland, one was a friend of Robert Burns. They developed chemical bleach to replace sun bleaching by spreading sheets and clothes on the grass (the green). After many trials and tribulations they succeeded and built what was in its time the biggest chemical plant in the world. The Bart became a multi-millionaire (equivalent to billionaire of today). He had 16 children and made a trust for each. They were naturally not too keen about their father marrying a second time but eventually she won them all over. When sister K was born brother Jack sent a telegram to brother Frank: "Another hundred thousand gone!" Although Mama inherited very little from her family she became very rich on her marriage and contributed greatly to our Lubbock/Tennant family, into which Peter and I were born. The Tennants were a Glasgow product of the Industrial Revolution.

LUBBOCK FAMILY

The Lubbock family is the product of the trade of the city of London. Our forebears built up a bank, Robarts Lubbock & Co, taken over by Coutts & Co after World War I. It was probably useful that they were mathematically minded. My great-grandfather Lubbock was awarded the Royal Medal for his mathematical work on tides. Our most illustrious forefather was my great uncle, the first Lord Avebury. He lived at High Elms next to Charles Darwin at Down House and was his protégé. Not only was he an important experimental biologist and a strong supporter of Darwinism, but he was also a banker (a bust of him resides in Coutts Bank in London) and, before elevation to the peerage, a Liberal MP who had originated 30 private members bills brought onto the statute book in his 30 years in the Commons. They varied from the preservation of bird life and plumage and what have you through to introducing a clearing bank system, the Ancient Monuments Act, and what erroneously became known as the Bank Holiday Act. It was thus: he felt strongly that families should be able to have holidays when they could all be together for that day. He said that there should be four such days in the year: Christmas, Easter, Whitsun and one more, and that one more should be the first Monday in August. A minor snag cropped up in that regarding the banking system of loans over a month - if the last day happened to be the first Monday in August, the system would be inoperable because everyone would be on holiday. There therefore had to be an amendment which just extended the time by one day if and when that situation ever arose. So that was just a banking problem and it stuck to the name of the Bank Holidays Act. His August bank holiday was known in the East

End of London as St. Lubbock's Day.[1] His life has been a guiding light to me. I am hoping that perhaps one of our grandsons will get the fire in his belly and contribute outstandingly to the great new world order which is almost within our reach today but is being hampered by disorder. With Boyd Orr and Avebury in their parentage, there is hope. And why not a grand-daughter as well as a grandson? The earliest reference to the family appears to be in the Eastern Counties (Norfolk). It probably came from the Hanseatic area, possibly Lübeck in Germany where I was held as a prisoner of war for short time in 1941. Thus we are Nordic and Celtic.

The above is the background from which I was nurtured. It may help you understand my behavior in life and for you to understand yourselves more. The Greeks had an injunction for people γνῶθι σεαυτόν, know yourself. This is sensible for your decision making for your lives.

My father joined the Boys' Brigade and then, when the Boer War started, he went out to South Africa to fight the Boers. When that war ended he came back to the Bank, Robarts, Lubbock and Company, in the city and the first day the staff stuck him on a chair and walked him round the block in praise of his return. At the turn of the century my father married my mother. My mother worshipped my father but she had had three children Peggy, Katharine and Nancy who were already in the household. There was a bad stepfather/stepdaughter relationship, he was not the Tennant type; another woman fell for my father. My mother just accepted this and brought it in to the family with great success. They all liked each other - this was noble of my mother and a sophisticated action except that Peggy, Katharine and Nancy, were never good to my father. My father died of a duodenal ulcer when I was at Cambridge. My mother died towards the end of World War II. I loved my father and my father loved me in a good father/son relationship. We had wonderful times in the holidays together. We were a sporting family. My mother loved any form of games or sport. We all came together very much in the game of golf.

My mother bore four daughters to her first husband, Sir Charles Tennant. The first was Peggy Wakehurst; the second was mentally defective. My mother, who was of course rich and could manage these things without financial strain, had this girl separated from the family and

---

[1]   His accomplishments have been referred to in the Notes and Records of the Royal Society and other journals as "The Forgotten Man", see appendix 2.

brought up in a house with, I believe, adequate nursing facilities to give her as good a life as possible under the circumstances. In this way my mother could devote her attention and love to the rest of the family without having to put the mentally disabled child first in all things and thereby really ruin the lives of her siblings. Today, in a family, if there is one that is mentally handicapped, the whole process of the life of the family is orientated around (distorted by?) trying to make the disabled child better. This means that the upbringing of the rest of the family becomes secondary to the care of the disabled child. Obviously there are pros and cons, but I know which I think is the better. The expense of treatment of the disabled child being kept at home will be almost as high.

My father had rather severe hammer toes and I was also born with hammer toes, though not so severely bad. The doctors told the family that I should go about barefoot as much as possible and I used to have to tuck lambs wool behind my bad toes when my feet were not bare. When I was asked to the Colquhouns at Rossdhu on Loch Lomond, first at about the age of 14 I think, I found that my host, Sir Iain Colquhoun walked about everywhere in bare feet. So naturally I thought this was a wonderful opportunity to emulate him. Through the winter I would wear shoes, but come the spring and holidays I would go barefoot. It would take about two days to get used to it and after that I could walk on rough stones, anything. Apart from the advantage to my hammer toes, it was a wonderful feeling to walk barefoot without pain. It is glorious in the Highlands - stalking, walking, shooting over the hill barefoot, and you were less tired. You get a sense of feeling through the feet - if you walk through sphagnum moss, it is a delight. You can tell quite a lot about the land when your feet are bare. When I came to farming at Farnell Mains I used to go about barefoot too. You can tell a lot about the condition of the soil. I even used to run over the stubble. But to let you into a secret, it is much easier to run over the stubble than to walk because as your foot goes down as you are running, it flattens the grain stalks and they don't stick into your foot!

I was once asked to shoot grouse walking up a hill by John Mackie at The Bent. He had six or seven guns I think and as we collected in the morning before moving off, one of the guns found he had come in slippers and had forgotten his shoes, so I asked what size of shoe he took and it was the same as mine. Now, I had brought a pair of shoes and was wearing them because it causes such a commotion if you start moving off with bare feet and people don't know about it. One does not want to draw attention to oneself in that way, but my feet were the same size so I just took my shoes off and gave them to this other chap and went on the shoot barefooted. They weren't very good shots but I was in the best form. We walked up the heather and I was bringing down birds right, left and centre and practically nobody else was! When we came back, people were a bit surprised and I was never asked to shoot there again - I can't think why! Years later I was in Edinburgh going to an exhibition of dolls' houses. Somebody came up behind me and said "What are you doing with your shoes on?" He had been down at a shoot at Ross Dhu with me and he recognised me and remembered my going barefoot! I never had any trouble with my hammer toes and they never developed into really bad hammer toes.

EPISODES

It is possible that some of the episodes of my life, especially those which caused an increased flow of adrenaline in the blood, may be of interest. I have had a charmed life having walked into and out of many scrapes. Perhaps there's a lesson to be learnt.

I was three years old when World War I, "The Great War", was declared. We had just gone to Dunvegan Castle. Daddy had taken it for this sporting season of August/September for three years. Daddy was called up to his North Somerset Yeomanry by telegram the night we arrived. The rest of the family were temporarily stuck there, but sister Margot whose husband was Herbert Henry Asquith sent us telegrams daily giving us news. (What price security?) We got to London after a time. We saw a Zeppelin dropping bombs over London but I don't remember it. I do remember Peter and me being put to bed in our house one night when there was a distant tremendous roar, and Mummy's face turned ashen. It was a munitions explosion in a big factory at Silverton in the East End of London. We could only get very little sugar and no butter, so we were not given any sugar as such at meals and we used "dripping" instead of butter.

Later we got up to North Berwick to our house, Glenconnor, which the Bart left to Mummy. Our house in the south of England, Greenhill, Warminster, Wilts, which my parents had bought after selling Broadoaks, they gave to the government for the duration for war use. It was made into a hospital for Australian wounded soldiers. They made such a mess of it that it was too expensive to restore. In London 31 Lennox Gardens, which the Bart had given Mummy and had been rented, became available. In the country we lived in a succession of houses, Jesmond Hill and Croft House, both of Pangbourne on the Thames near Reading, and finally Birch Hall,

Windlesham, Surrey. The latter Mummy left Peter who sold it when we were in Washington, D.C.

At North Berwick, where we stayed toward the end of the war, we used to see aircraft and "blimps" guarding the Firth of Forth. These were airships lifted by hydrogen in three long bags attached together like a bunch of three bananas with the gondola below. These used to fly over the house at about 800 feet. It was partly seeing these that started my interest in flying. Later this was increased after being taken through the airship R34 in her hanger at East Fortune by Capt. Irwin R.N. who flew her across the Atlantic and back.

Daddy, who had served in the Boer war as a boy, was wounded by shrapnel in the Great War at the Ypres front in 1917. Unfit to return to his regiment in Europe he was assigned to Dublin to command a unit to help cope with the uprisings.

After the war we were able to return to Dunvegan for the sporting seasons of 1919 and 1920. The MacLeod of MacLeod generously allowed my father to defer the remaining two years of the contract to postwar. He shared it with his cavalry friend Sir Archibald Langman and both families had a glorious time there. Sister Peggy became engaged to John Loder there, and it was there that I fell in love with the West Coast of Scotland.

Brother Peter and I went to day school in London at Mr. Gibbs in Sloane Street for a year before going to a private boarding school, Naish House at Burnham-on-Sea Somerset. We called it Burnham-on-Mud because of the stone sized lumps of mud there on the beach. These were supposed to be good for Peter's asthma.

Peter then went to Eton to F.W. Dobbs' house but the climate was too damp for his health. He had to leave after one half (term) and went to college on the Lake of Geneva.

F.W. Dobbs was the first person apart from my father and our Nanny Skinner to make a constructive effort in my life. My father made his on me by association, he was very fond of me as I of him and we did much together. Dobbs, M'tutor, I grew to respect during my time at Eton and after.

Francis Wellesley Dobbs was a younger twin whose home was Castle Dobbs on the north coast of the Lough of Belfast. They were identical twins and when his elder brother came to stay at Jourdalay's, the Eton

College house, he used sometimes to come round to our bedrooms in the evening to say good night. We couldn't tell the difference between them and you can imagine the fun he had confusing us!

M'tutor had a great mind especially mathematical. He used to race the provost Monty James (M.R. James OM, author of texts on ancient manuscripts and of a popular classic, "Ghost Stories of an Antiquary") to finish the first acrostic (forerunner of crossword) by Torquemada. It required a high level of erudition and imagination and could not always be finished for days. Anyway, if any of his house was the subject of a complaint by any other Master, his immediate reaction was a defense of the boy. He would discuss the misdemeanors with the perpetrator and if the boy had thought out what he was doing, even if it was against regulations or even wrong, he would be lenient. But heaven help him if he said he didn't think. His was the best of Irish attitudes. He was proud of his boys and we were proud of him.

ETON COLLEGE

There has been so much written about Eton. I would say a major feature is that over the years it has struck a wonderful balance between developing the soul of a boy and gregariousness - how to behave in a crowd, en masse, as one of a group. There is an example here, right now. My grandson, who is there, has taken to rowing. He is doing pretty well and he loves it and he is winning races in the school house games. But he is also a fast runner and he has been running for Eton College against other schools in the UK. Now he will have to give up one or the other in order to be good enough at a single sport. He will decide which. I rather think, in many other so-called public schools, the decision would be made for him.

Of course the family of Lubbock have had connections with Eton College for a century or more - probably two centuries. Their best known activities were on the athletics side. The Eton Ramblers Cricket Club was started by my great uncles who were choosing a ghastly colour for a Club tie when my great aunt Harriet, their sister, refused to let them have it. They said, all right, you choose and she produced the one which is really rather lovely and one sees it being worn in many society places in London. You could be either a "dry" bob or a "wet" bob - i.e. play cricket or row in the summer, and one Lubbock was captain of the cricket eleven and rowed in the Eton eight. This was also exemplified in a smaller way by my father. He was a dry bob and in the finals of the house cricket competition he bowled out the opposing side for something like 58 runs - anyway it was a fantastic effort and remembered for many years. From Eton he went to Trinity College, Oxford and there he rowed and they had fours rowing at Henley Regatta for the Visitors Cup which my father rowed in and they won the cup. But it wasn't all athletics. When I was at Eton there was a Housemaster there, Samuel Gurney Lubbock who was a Greek scholar and there were Lubbock writers and authors that developed from Eton. One or two Lubbocks, when they left Eton, went to Cambridge and stayed on as Dons and became Heads of Cambridge Colleges. The great John Lubbock, Lord Avebury, left Eton at the age of 15, I think, to go and help his father in the Bank - Robarts, Lubbock and Company. So he didn't get so far at Eton although I believe he went there at a very early age, earlier than they do nowadays.

MY "LOVE-LIFE"

I think one has to face up to recording one's love life because it is an important aspect of one's being. I fell deeply in love at the age of 21. Not only was I in love with her, but I was very fond of her family and this made it difficult to pursue the line of all being fair in love and war. Anyway, my love was unrequited and from then on I just avoided young females. I suppose I was what you might call an eligible young man. It so happened that in the London summer society when I was at Cambridge I was asked to all sorts of dances and balls in London to which I went just to have a good time and see lots of people, but not to be looking out for a girl. Suddenly I would see that some mother had arranged a party with me sitting down to dinner next to her daughter and that I was being expected to at least take an interest in her. It just made me boil with rage and I ran away from it as fast as I possibly could.

Anyway, after that, having finished with Cambridge and London high society, and moved to the Rowett Institute in Aberdeen I began to find my place.

MINTY

The change came in a miraculous fashion. Suddenly I saw a brilliant star in Minty Orr, lovely in every way, with a father the greatest Scot of the 20th century and a mother even cleverer. She was born with everything, then at the age of four, five or six came what was probably German Measles and a very lowered resistance involving the need to operate on her ears. Her parents had agreed to the operation which was carried out by an Aberdeen surgeon. I don't know if I should say this or not, but he was called by the students "Septic Sandy" because he always believed that a little sepsis left behind was good to keep up the resistance to disease. Her father and mother had discussed whether or not to have her tonsils taken out at the same time and ended up very strongly against having them taken out. Somehow this was not made clear because Sandy, when he came out from the theatre said that everything had gone well and, by the way, I took her tonsils out. I believe Minty's father's face turned green. She was left with absolutely no hearing in one ear and very little in the other. I believe her life hung in the balance for some months. In the early days it must have been like being in prison. There were no suitable hearing aids and she could only hear if somebody spoke very close to the ear with residual hearing. Yet, here she was, bonny and blithe. With Boyd Orr's help, we became engaged.

She then went to England to learn lip-reading. There she met what proved to be a life-long friend, Cicily Shear. Cicily married another deaf boy, Pip, and the two of them have lived together ever since, married and working in a pharmacy. We seldom see each other now, but remain life-long friends.

Back in Wardenhill she went to the "Do" School, The School of Domestic Science in Aberdeen. There she had a hilarious time. She had been to school, but it was only in name. She sat and read her own books when nobody was looking. At the Do School she made a close friend of Lindsey who married George Mackie later.

Now, I have noticed that if you are blind, many people are likely to consider you to be of above average intelligence; but if you are deaf, you are considered to be stupid. So what could this great intellect do, not able to hear, not having been educated? How was she to communicate and express herself? The answer was through art. She went to Grays School of Art in Aberdeen and learned to paint and to sculpt. She adored it and, of course, this was the outlet for her talents. I encouraged her to sculpt because I could see how beautifully she could communicate her feelings for and of someone through modelling a head with her hands. Through this medium she could express herself in a wonderful way. She became brilliant as a sculptress. She was able to give life to a head and an unbelievable likeness in an incredibly short time. Mostly she did portraits because that was what people commissioned, but her statuettes were superb. She exhibited in the Paris Salon and in London at the Royal Academy as well as fairly regularly in Aberdeen and Edinburgh. She never had an agent and her mastery of sculpture has gone practically unrecognised; but that was not her way and she has always underestimated the value of her work. But the stardom is there for posterity through the work she has done in modelling, and her great talent for art has been an outlet for her brilliance. At the same time she created a family of four and brought them all up beautifully as well as being a loving wife.

My going to America to work at FAO brought her into a totally new world. She met people of high intellect comparable with her own and when we had cocktail parties she flourished because she was able to move about and hear as opposed to having formal lunch parties or dinner parties where everything was agony to her. She couldn't hear anything of the person sitting on her left and the jumble of voices made it very difficult for her to hear the person on her right, or any of the other conversation around her. So she became what the family called "The Martini Queenie!"

I have always been hard on her because I never wanted our love to become lowered to a level of my being sentimental and over-protective towards her. It wouldn't have worked that way but I have often been inconsiderate. I have always felt that I had a call to work to try to improve the feeding of peoples and it has pretty well always taken precedence. Yet, through it all, we have kept our love for each other and made happy lives, sometimes against great odds.

It was one day when a group of us was on the beach at Aberdeen I realised that there was a girl in the party that was making for me, if you can put it that way. I knew I was not interested but it flipped me over quite suddenly into realising that I had fallen in love with Minty and no one else. No other woman was to count for the rest of my days. She has a heart of gold, mind of diamond, health destroyed by medical errors, courage of lion to overcome them, always helping lame ducks by the score, self-expression by sculpture of superb quality. She is the cleverest of us all. There is, of course, no-one like her.

She produced Ann Pat 12 days after I was shot down and had become a prisoner of war. Her existence was a great solace to both of us, separated between Scotland and Germany. Minty presented her to me nearly four years later when I came back from the war. Then she produced a succession of three sons, all born in Washington DC in the height of the summer. You are the ones for which this is written; you are the ones who wanted to know "What did you do in World War II, Daddy and what did you do before and after?" This is my jumbled answer.

Loving someone, I believe, begins gradually. Other people see when one is starting to be in love before one knows it oneself and then suddenly the moment comes. And that is why it is called falling in love. It happens suddenly that you become aware of it and it reorientates the whole of your vision of life. It happened to me on the beach bathing near Aberdeen. From then on I knew that our lives were locked together. I meant to marry her above all things.

When Douglas Bader was asked by a friend shortly after Brickhill's biography of Douglas "Reach for the Sky", how did he, Douglas, feel? He answered "Bloody naked, old boy". If one is to leave a fairly true impression, and I don't think one can do more than that, one has to strip naked.

****

First Sunday in August, 1992.

My great niece, Sarah Van Hove, over from Brussels with one of her children, Laura, has come all this way to see us for two days. Then Bob and Jane Wenlock and Bob's mother came to lunch on their way to Shetland.

I lost out badly: I had an agenda of things I wanted Bob to do. Bob came in and sat down and announced that he was on holiday and could do nothing. He then proceeded to explain why I, poor little I, was the only person in the world who could help to unravel the food consumption surveys for the 1930s. I had always meant to do this when I came back from the war but the call to go to start up the Food and Agricultural Organisation seemed a stronger message. Also, in those days, it did not seem to matter so much. What has happened now is that new techniques and new information have shown that malnutrition in pregnancy and in the first years of life can affect the heart and lead to diseases 40 or 50 years later, so the data that we collected on people - their names, addresses, ages and food consumption - has suddenly become of enormous value if you can get it. Well, it is there in black and white but parts of it have been worked on in Southampton University and Bristol, I think, and it is all higgledy-piggledy. The only thing I can do is to try,[2] if they can get someone to pull it all together, to answer the whys and the wherefores, and to fill in the gaps in the information which would make it important to select or reject data that are lying in the records: so I reckon I have got to keep myself alive a long time now.

I never recognised until today that one can't have a completely private life. Just by being you are part of public property. Let's hope that it is a good St. Lubbock's Day in Newton of Stracathro tomorrow.

It will be wonderful if the December UN meeting makes a stand for the New World Order starting with a World Food Authority with powers to co-ordinate activities other than agriculture, fisheries etc. I am afraid that my mind goes round and round on the old thoughts and the old sayings that have been in our minds for 20, 30, 40 years and now I am only too happy that the lead is being taken by Philip James - Director of the Rowett Research Institute, *fons et origo* as far as I'm concerned. I hope to be able to thrust my oar in from time to time, but that would only be to try to steady the boat not steer it. Now I am beginning to feel myself free to talk about my life.

****

---

[2]   See p.80, "The Carnegie Survey."

"SPORTSMAN"

It's a nasty thing isn't it! In rowing I was either a good second-class oar or a bad first-class oar - I alone or with others never won the top prizes. This is probably a good thing - I think that I learnt a lot more by almost winning the Visitors at Henley, running into the booms and losing the last race: that sort of thing. I learnt a lot about life that I would never have learnt if I had been all that successful. I would just have been proud and rather arrogant! Anyway, my son, Geoffrey, won races at Henley Regatta and now grandchildren are coming up starting to learn to row and succeeding rather well.

Making a boat skim through the water, when in an eight you have got all eight working absolutely together in perfect timing - I think that is perhaps the highlight of physical satisfaction in competition. Next to that was the great enjoyment of being a sportsman. It was the greatest joy to go out to Switzerland and to Austria to ski. There, in the same way, if you got your balance working perfectly you come down a mountain side turning at the right moment and keeping your balance - an achievement which has an enormous thrill.

At home I enjoyed fishing and shooting. If the ecologists wishing to maintain the balance of this and that animal were to manage them as well as the sportsmen have their fishing and shooting of partridges, pheasants and the like, they would manage to keep a balance of life and look after the species in a way that has not so far, to my knowledge, come up to the sportsman's standards.

As far as marksmanship is concerned, shooting on the hills taught me a lot about shooting at moving objects. When it came to the Fleet Air Arm and we were given trials at shooting at a drogue being towed by another aeroplane, moving forward, dropping back etc. we all had test shots to see what we could do, and it was easy for me; they could not really believe how my percentage of hits was so much higher than the rest of the squadron - that was why. Nevertheless, it did not help in the end because my air gun was shot to pieces before I could use it when my air gunner was killed.

Coming to wartime, I don't suppose my experiences were much different from anyone else's, nor can one ever describe one's experiences for other people who have not been through the trauma of prison in a way that they can understand it. I joined up with 828 Squadron. After final training at Condor in Arbroath we were sent down to Greenwich for a short time where we were given some nice meals to teach us how to hold knives and forks in our hands properly!

But before getting that far, I want to come back to a little titbit about shooting on the hill and Ann Pat's schooling. When we went to America, we took her with us. We were there for five years, so she was then about 9 years old and needing to get into school in Scotland on our return. I asked around as to which were the better schools and to my horror found that all the private ones were booked up. However, sister K wrote to Elizabeth Lyle, daughter of Archie Sinclair who had been Minister for Air during the war. She wrote and asked if Elizabeth could possibly squeeze Ann Pat into her school. The Lyles had three daughters and a long way to go to any school, so they started teaching them themselves, then with a governess and then gradually developed it into a little school; it has been successful and continues on a larger scale to this day. Elizabeth wrote to say she was terribly sorry, but she really hadn't got a bed for her. The following day K was rung up by Elizabeth who asked, "Does David still eat boiled eggs with the shell on?" The rapid reply was, "Of course", whereupon Elizabeth said, "I think we can find a corner in the house and take Ann Pat in" - and that started her education in Scotland, apart from pre-school education in Aberdeen when she was three years old.

Somehow I never seemed to think about myself as an "individual". It was years later when somebody said "Oh, don't you know you were considered the strongest man in Cambridge"? - I hadn't the faintest idea. I may have thought bare feet were a little eccentric, but for me that was just a good thing, and that was that. Somebody described me many years later on the Muc Mhara, sailing on the West Coast, as tough. I never thought of myself as tough. After that I did check back and remembered that Walter Elliot had said to Orr that on David's boat you were lucky if you were given an anchor for a pillow.

Putting things down on paper like this might make it appear that I was a "poseur" - in reality I was quite the opposite. I was just me!

I never really had much pleasure in the stalking, except for the walking. If you have killed a stag and prepared it for eating, a feeling of achievement was certainly based on a blood lust. What I found was that if I went stalking (usually by myself, although I had a boy down the hill somewhere with a mountain pony who would come up and carry the stag away) and the stalk had been exciting and I had struggled through hillside burns and turned myself upside down in order not to be seen and so on, if I had had a real contest and won, there was a good feeling about it - or anyway a nice feeling. But if I came across a stag which was an easy shot, I would try and get it but I would always miss! There was no blood lust and I felt too sorry for the stag.

Boyd Orr said to Walter Elliot, when I started up at the Rowett, we must educate him and this made Walter laugh loud and long: he thought that a boy who had been to school at Eton and had come through Cambridge was educated. Not my father-in-law, and my father-in-law was right! I didn't know about people as people. I didn't know the fishermen in Peterhead in a close fashion. When I was sailing I would sail into fishing harbours and talk with the men and have a good time with them, but that wasn't really knowing them. With nearly all people, if you really know them and their background you can get on with them. In those days the natural group behaviour of the Scots people towards foreigners was embarrassingly generous. If I were to anchor in any loch and then get out the dinghy and row ashore, I would be met probably by the wife tending her animals and vegetables around the croft, but she would have already picked her best cabbages, or potatoes or whatever to give to me. It was wonderful, but I couldn't repay her and in a way it kept us apart. I remember once sailing into Loch Duich past Eilean Donan Castle and anchoring. We caught some rather good fish and we took some and somewhat sheepishly presented the fish to the farmer's wife, as we thought, but she spoke with a broad Glasgow accent. She was simply delighted with the fish because she said she couldn't get any, being so far from the sea! They had just arrived for a fortnight's holiday. That worked - but I couldn't do it successfully on a general basis.

LUBBOCK, TENNANT, DUGDALE STORIES

Once we were going up North and approaching the Kyle of Lochalsh and there were some narrows and high tidal streams on the way there about 10 miles off. It was a very calm day and so we had to use the engine. But alas and alack the carburettor jet blocked at a very crucial moment trying to get through the stream. A whale steamer was coming by and I asked to have a tow and he towed us a couple of miles into harbour to the east and then carried on his way. Of course, he knew who I was and I was able to thank him later on. But I had to anchor for a bit and there was more to be done with the engine so my crew, which was Peggy and Katharine (not Nancy I don't think) went into the hotel at the head of the loch and had some tea or high tea. Peggy, who was always interested in people (in that sense, she was the most widely educated person I know) got talking with the proprietor who seemed to have a wider degree of education than one would have expected. When I had got things in the engine righted, and we were able to move off and get safely to the Kyle of Lochalsh, Peggy told us what she had found which was that the proprietor was a n'er-do-well brother of Frank Tennant's wife. She had another brother who was a Government authority on coal mining, a man who had acquitted himself well in life. However, when Annie Redmayne became engaged to Frank Tennant a deal was made whereby the n'er-do-well was bought off and signed some document. [Annie Redmayne was the daughter of John Marnike Redmayne, an alkali manufacturer.] Peggy had a natural interest in people and the ability to find out the interesting things about people's lives.

Frank Tennant was the youngest surviving son of old Sir Charles Tennant. Frank was in charge of the soap-making division of the Charles

Tennant company bleach industry. They had a partner of the name of Ogsten from Aberdeen [Colonel James Ogsten known as 'soapy Ogsten'] and the soap that was produced was Ogsten and Tennants. When I was a child I didn't know there was any other type of soap for all that we ever had was Ogsten and Tennants soap - and very good it was too! Old Sir Charles Tennant had decreed that my mother's household should have Ogsten and Tennant's soap free of charge for the rest of her life. Like all these things, it didn't last because the business was sold off to ICI who failed to honour the arrangement - as if it mattered very much.

Any of the Tennant family who wanted action would come to my mother for help. Jack Tennant ran his political campaign for Berwickshire, [later renamed Berwick and Haddington] from my mother's house, Glenconnor, North Berwick. Lucy Graham Smith [neé Tennant], who was a very fine painter and a great friend of my mother's, couldn't manage to get up to Scotland as she was crippled, but she used to come to us in our house at Windlesham. Prime Minister Herbert Henry Asquith and his wife Margot, née Tennant used to come and stay for relaxation from time to time. They usually rented some larger place for themselves so that they could continue with the business of government during recess. Eddy Tennant, the oldest surviving son, became the second Baronet and then was ennobled and took the name of Glenconnor which of course tied things back to the south west of Scotland from which the Tennants came.

Of course the family were, when they first heard, annoyed with their father for marrying again. But with the rather magical technique of my mother's they all came round and they came to depend on her and to love her. During the comparatively short time of my mother's life as wife of Sir Charles Tennant she produced for him four girls - one died in adolescence. Nancy Dugdale of Crathorne, the youngest, died of cancer twenty years ago or so and Dame Peggy Wakehurst and Baroness Elliot are still alive, now 92 and 85 respectively I think. The oldest is getting very blind now, although she never says a word about it. She is an angel - Minty and I adore her and she reciprocates. She sits in 31 Lennox Gardens in London and she looks after all her extended family of Loders and Reeder-Harrises and Van Hoves. They all come to share their difficulties with her and to listen to her advice, and generally to take it.

My sister Nancy's first marriage was to Sylvester Gates and did not last long. He was brilliant but he was also a sadist. Nancy met Tommy [Dugdale, later Lord Crathorne] at K's wedding at North Berwick. Tommy had been in the same regiment as Walter and was I think his Best Man. Tommy was a delightful Yorkshire squire. His father was very rich, making his money mostly out of the merging of the Cunard and White Star steamship companies with which he built an enormous house outside the village of Crathorne. There are 20, 30 bedrooms - I don't know what! Nancy and I were very close all the time after her divorce and before her marriage to Tom. Nancy and I were motoring from London, where we shared a house, to North Berwick. We were slowed up and didn't get as far as we had intended to, and the question was where we should spend the night. I said that I knew a family called Johnson - Maurice was a contemporary school chum of mine so I rang up his parents and they were delighted to put us up for the night. As we arrived or were approaching Crathorne Nancy looked across a ravine to a house on a cliff and said that is an enormous monster of a house - and I said, it belongs to some people called Dugdale who are the owners of the house which the Johnsons rent. This must have been a year or two before K's wedding. After the wedding Tom and Nancy got to know each other and to fall in love with one another and they got married. We stayed at the Grange which the Johnsons were renting. Tommy Dugdale, who was old enough to fight at the end of World War I, felt guilt about the riches that his father had made from the merger and so he thought he should contribute to the commonweal. He stood for parliament and got in as a Conservative for Richmond, North Yorkshire. At all general elections he was returned with vast majorities. He got let down by his civil servants and others in the government when he was Minister of Agriculture over some property which the government was holding on to but which was contested by the people who owned it previously. They said that the arrangement was that after the war, when things had settled down, they would be given back the farm and the land. Anyway, Tommy had to go on with the data he got from his department. The story became clearer that government were wrong about the ownership of the place, Critchell Down, and it should go back to the previous owner and because of his mistake, Tommy was resigning forthwith. He went on working as Chief Whip and he was one of the most influential members of parliament, carrying out his duties assiduously. When the day for giving honours came round, Tommy was elevated to the peerage and took the name of Crathorne, the place where he was brought up.

He was a greatly respected member of parliament and had many friends in all parties. He was a great horseman, he won many competitions and many races. His father's stable was built up for high speed, flat racing. Early on in his youth he won numbers of steeplechases. His judgement compared favourably with anybody else's. After Nancy's first marriage failed I spent a good deal of time with her. We shared a house together in London, Bedford Gardens. Naturally I withdrew but only gradually because Tommy, instead of wanting me out of the way, rather liked to have me in the way. He bought Nancy a beautiful Bentley. Nancy's comment was "David will love this" - somewhat to his chagrin, but nevertheless, he thought it extremely amusing. Walter Elliot and Tommy were friends from World War I days when they were in the same regiment. Walter took Tommy for his Best Man at the wedding in North Berwick. One basked in the sunshine of Walter's company.

****

(Tomorrow David Dugdale, my godson, is coming up from Yorkshire and goes back again the same day - noble man!)

****

SAILING

My father loved sailing as his father did before him. I never heard about it but my father and grandfather must have sailed around in boats on the west coast of Scotland at one time. They presumably will have taken holiday time off from the Bank - Robarts, Lubbock and Co. - and taken a summer holiday sailing and sea fishing. Anyway, he wanted me to share some of that enjoyment of the sea so he wrote to the harbour master at East Loch Tarbert and asked him to pick out of the fishing fleet there some decent sailing, fishing vessel which was well-made and would not let us down. Accordingly a 1909 lugsail-rigged herring boat was selected. It was registered as Tarbert I - she was called "The Annie" and was very well-known in the fishing world of that type of boat. That year my father had taken a shoot near the Kyles of Bute and the boat was brought up there.

My father had arranged a reconstruction - instead of going down a hatch to a well full of fish, he had the deck cleared off leaving an open well where we could sit sailing either low down so we couldn't see the water or higher up on either side to enjoy the waves and the breeze. It had an engine. It was a Kelvin one cylinder paraffin engine, but the engine wound up backwards - which foxed most people trying to help! - and there was no gear box so that when you wound the engine to get it started, the propeller began turning immediately and only moved the boat forward! If you were anchored and you were in a slipway tidal race, you had to look very slippy to shorten the anchor chain, get down into the engine hold, start the engine, dash back to the bow and pull up the anchor. Unless you had somebody with you, you might be going all over the place because there was nobody to steer. This seemed to me to be all good clean fun but the parents and friends of their age advised us not to carry on with this. Eventually we replaced this single cylinder Kelvin with a two cylinder paraffin Kelvin with a gear box which, when pushed forward, would move the boat forward and when pulled right back, reversed the propeller; there was a neutral gear in between. This was luxury! [Minty added in the margin: There was confusion in Oban harbour when you told Minty "Pull it back" from the cabin. So I pulled it back, it went into reverse and had to be manoeuvred backwards through the fishing boats until neutraled!]

The first year I had Guy Burgess teaching me. The next year my father took a stalking forest just north of Mallaig, the Knoydart Estate. In the intervening winter and until the war, it was looked after by the Smith brothers who had a yard in Tighnabruaich in the Kyles of Bute. They were notorious as the dirtiest shinty players in Argyll - however they were very good to me! They were instructed to bring the boat, "The Annie", up to Oban and my father and I alone would sail her up to Mallaig. However, my father went down with a terrible 'flu-type infection and we only just managed to fit it in. We stayed in the major hotel in Oban until he was nearly fit and then we sailed her up and got into Mallaig. We didn't have a compass; we didn't have a chart; we had a road map! In Mallaig we bought provisions for the house on the Knoydart promontory where, I hoped, I was going to grass stags. So next day we sailed into the Loch just north of Mallaig (Loch Nevis?) where we were warned about one or two things. For example, there was a very steep cliff on the south side and when the wind was blowing strongly, it would cause cats' paws, spinning round picking up water from the surface of the sea. When I began to look further into this matter of sailing and navigating, I got the "West Coast Pilot" which was an admirable book written in perfect English - it would have been dangerous to have had any ambiguity in the instructions. The book said on the entrance to this loch, great care should be taken: some of the rocks were still uncharted, the whirlwinds could cause great damage to any sailing vessel and people should take the utmost care for "loss of life is not uncommon"!

Stalking was rather fun; I would take somebody with me and sail round the Knoydart point, land with my rifle and start stalking from that end of the forest, working my way south and getting home on foot. Well, one day I grassed a stag and I started to head home. I got a keeper to take the highland pony out and put the stag on to be carried back. The wind was blowing great guns and the rain was pelting down and I was very cold.

After I had seen to everything I thought necessary and I was no longer needed, I ran back to the house we were in. I had a bath and cleaned up and in those days I expect I put on a dinner jacket, white collar and black tie, etc. The wind was getting stronger. My father and mother wanted to know what sort of a day I had had and I was telling them what happened when one of the boys in the place came haring into the dining room and said "The boat has gone", so I guessed that it had dragged anchor. I knew the direction of the wind so thought I could pick it up and bring it back in, anchoring it with a couple of anchors and it should then be all right. So I asked for a volunteer to row out in a rowing boat with me and we would scour the sea in the direction in which the boat must of gone, find it and get on board and then bring it back.

I had asked for a rowing boat to be got ready whilst I was changing my clothes. When I got down to the beach there were three men who helped to push us off and I started rowing. There was water coming over the gunwales which wasn't surprising when the storm was so high but I began to notice that the boat was filling with water fairly rapidly so I told my companion to bale, which he did in a rather lackadaisical fashion, I felt - although actually I think that he was scared stiff. Anyway, despite all his efforts with the baler, the boat was filling up with water faster than he was being able to take water out. I looked towards him but could see nothing as it was pitch black - "Did you put the bung in?" I asked. "The bung?" he said. And then I realised. "Look", I said, "a boat like this has a hole in the keel for draining the water out of it when lying on the beach so that the timbers are not warped by the weight of the water". Then I said "Can you swim?" Afterwards there was a difference in the fervour of activity! I said "You've got to hunt round in the bottom of the boat until you get your hands on the bung and then put it in the hole at the bottom of the boat and then bale out further". Meanwhile I went on rowing out to sea and eventually we got to "The Annie". I tied up over the stern and we both got into the boat and I got the engine started and we moved in towards the land and found a place for anchoring. I put out two anchors - a Kedge with the regular one - and I deemed that safe and we came ashore.

Years afterwards I was told that in a competition in the Daily Express for the most frightening time you have ever had in your life, this lad gave a description of this incident and it was taken and printed.

Of course the stories are legion of the boat and there came into the picture the Chieftain, Sir Iain Colquhoun of Luss who loved sailing and came with me many, many years. We none of us liked "The Annie" for a name and he chose a Gaelic couple of words "Mhuc Mara" which is literally "Sea Pig" as used to describe the whale. She was something of a whale. He and Sir John Gilmore, Bart, of Montrave were my most common companions. The latter kept something a diary or log of the voyages each year that he made with me and it is very well done. He is a great character and I am very fond of him. (If any of you are interested, you could perhaps ask to have a copy made.)

It was enormous fun and one year we were down at Oronsay, the island south of Colonsay. We made a plan to sail over to Northern Ireland and collect Charles Fletcher. Well, the best laid plans were going awry. There was a force nine storm for two or three days. If we did not go and pick him up in time, it would not have been worth his coming over and so it was a matter of going at the first available opportunity. I took advice from a sea captain we should not go. I said, "Yes, I agree it's not the best of times, but we'll pull through all right won't we?" "Yes" he said, "you will". So sister K, Ivor Colquhoun (Iain Colquhoun's son) and I set out for Northern Ireland on the day when the weather started to ease up. Of course, that is the worst day for the sea because as the wind eases up, so the sea rises up and the cross-currents in the north of Ireland cause what is called a "confused sea". We were heading to cross and I didn't think the weather was good enough, so we turned into the Rinns of Islay to take shelter for the night and then carry on. This we did and it was successful, but when we tackled it the next day, as on the previous evening, the confused sea consisted of cauldron-shaped waters so that your sailing boat and your sails came out of the wind when you were in the bottom of the cup and then when you pushed up to the edge the wind pretty well flattened you because you had no way of controlling the boat. Sister K couldn't hold the tiller, it was too hard for her. She was very strong. Ivor lay sick in the bottom of the boat mostly, so I had the boat to run by myself which was nice!

We got over and we saw the Fletcher family and picked up Charles and started back for Oronsay. The wind had gone and the mist had rolled up. Now, the south end of Oronsay is just one mass of reefs like stark, cutting fingers sticking out to the south. I was frightened - I suppose the visibility was 15 to 20 yards and if I hadn't got my navigation right, we'd have had some trouble! Luckily we made quite a good landfall and got into the anchorage in Oronsay. When we crossed the strand from Oronsay to Colonsay and went to the one shop by the harbour the proprietor turned a vivid green colour - he was sure we could never have survived such weather and we must be ghosts!

Luss [Sir Iain] found sailing with me was the best relaxation that he could ever come across, so he said. He would come sailing with me every summer. He had the DSO and Bar and was three times recommended for a VC and never got it. The reason was that he had been court martialed for fraternising with the enemy. On Christmas Day he had organised a football match in no man's land with the Germans in the lines opposite his. All went off extremely well and both sides were very happy about it all. They returned back into their trenches and thought what fun. Unfortunately there are no photographs of this - there was great excitement, lots of snaps were taken but there wasn't film! Of course there had been trouble like this the previous year and there had been an edict that it was not to happen again, so he was well in the wrong, but he felt it was well worth doing. That's a Scots Chieftain for you! He was court martialed and condemned to death. The King, George V, quashed the results of the court martial and gave him back his right to live. I asked what happened next and he said "nothing really" because he had been in the front line the next day. It didn't worry him except later the Chairman, or whatever he was called, of the Court Martial Board was Lord Caban and he never spoke to Sir Iain Colquhoun again. If they met in a club, he would turn away from him.

Iain and the King got on very well together, not unnaturally. He used to ask Iain up every year to stay at Balmoral to suggest various ways for improving the stock of deer at on the estate. He would partake in the shooting of hinds etc. and a number of days of straight stalking, I think. I only ever saw them together once and that was at the launching of the Queen Mary from Brown's dockyard in the Clyde. There, as at other public meetings, the King took an early opportunity to make a heavy joke about his saving Iain's life, but there really was friendship between the two men. I recognised it when at Rossdhu one evening - I was very young then - Dinah was in bed and they wanted me in: I sat on the bed and Iain sat on a chair at a table writing letters. Dinah said "Who have you got to write to?" and he said "I want to write to the King" just as if it was to Marks and Spencer. Iain, of course, was Lord Lieutenant of Dumbartonshire. He spoke the Gaelic and must have been the Commissioner of the police amongst other things, but he was always looking after the police and the police were always coming to him for advice about different things. If I was driving him somewhere, we would stop at the side of the road because there was a friend of his on point duty. I was driving him through Glasgow one day. I didn't know the direction or where to go and we came to a cross-roads of five or six roads together and he got confused and said: turn left, no right, not left .... I got in a thorough muddle and the policeman, who was in the centre, stopped all the traffic, signalled to me to go to the side of the road which I did and then he came over to give lecture me, I suppose. He looked in and saw that Luss was in the car, so he just said "I'm sorry to have held you up, drive on!" - at least that is how it was translated from the Gaelic to me.

Iain was 30 years older than me. My father-in-law was 30 years older than me. By working with Boyd Orr my colleagues were all mostly 30 years older than me, but providing we had an interest in common objectives, age differences never bothered me at all. I fell in love with Minty Orr who was eight years younger than me and here we are together 52 years later with a bunch of wonderful families, all gathered together today with the exception of Moira, John Angus and Julia who are house-sitting in Marblehead for Geoffrey and family.

By the fireside in Iain's room at his home on Rossdhu on Rossdhu Sound there used to hang a wood club with an iron ring with earwiggled teeth on it, 18" to 2' long. There was also a damaged revolver. The revolver had a live shell still in it, but the damage prevented it from being taken out. The story is this: his Unit had been brought into action the day before in a most ill-conceived manoeuvre as a result of which they were decimated and Iain lost a great number of his very close friends. He went berserk. I think he had to be taken out of the lines and given some medical attention because he was so mad with rage. He was about 5'5" tall, had a little military moustache and his normal dress was the kilt. He was the most enormous fun to be with. His knowledge of all things of the country was immense. He had an enchanting sense of humour. He loved me as if I were his son in the same way as Boyd Orr loved me. We used to go sailing with his children all over the west coast and we would stop from time to time and camp on land. It was an ideal kind of holiday atmosphere, having the fun of sailing sometimes in good weather, sometimes in very bad, but always wonderful.

I also had a number of sailing companions: Geoffrey Burge, my stockbroker who was a very good sailor with a lovely yacht - his father's originally, in the south of England, but it came to him; "Shuffles" Hopwood who became a general in the army with considerable merit - I believe he had a wonderful career; Terrance Sanders, Dean of Corpus Christi, Cambridge; Eric Powell whose tank received a direct hit in World War II and exploded; Kenneth Payne, one of the leading oarsmen of his day; Mike Tennant, Iain's brother-in-law - Iain was married to Dinah Tennant, daughter of brother Frank, i.e. one of the offspring of Sir Charles Tennant, the father of Peggy, K and Nancy.

Usually, when the vacations started, I motored up north with a team probably to Rossdhu where we congregated and Iain used to say that every year I produced larger and stronger, more vigorous men for my crew. Then we used to go by Clyde steamer and end up in Tighnabruaich and we would take the Mhuc from there and sail round the Mull of Kintyre or through the Crinan Canal. In those days it was so leaky that in a decent summer it dried out and you couldn't get through. We'd sail off somewhere and then some of the crew would have to go home and I would get others following up so that, if possible, we always had three people to manage the Mhuc. At the end of the vacation we would sail her back to anchorage in Smith's yard in Tighnabruaich. Years later the Smith brothers used to look with great relief when they saw Mhuc Mara returning because she was a very old boat and they thought she wasn't going to stand up to the rigours to which I put her. But she was a fine boat and a friend. Sailing in her I felt at one with her and with the sea.[3]

---

[3]   Tailpiece on sailing: Sir Godfrey Collins [Secretary of State for Scotland 1932-36] at my mother's request made me promise to take a lifebelt with me when we were going sailing. Well I took a belt, not that there seemed much point. When we came back at the end of our cruise and we were packing up at Tighnabruaich, we threw the lifebelt overboard. A few bubbles came slowly to the surface as the lifebelt sank to the bed of the sea.

FLYING

The following is a story on its own and a commentary on air travel: "Aeroplanes, Flying Boats and Zeppelins or Lighter-Than-Air Craft"

When I was Secretary of the Scientific Society at Eton College where we members would write papers and present them to meetings amongst ourselves, I decided to write about the coming airship which was then called the R101. This part is political: it was decided by the Labour Party which was then in power that they would show the superiority of national state production versus private enterprise. The Ministry of Air was to be responsible for the production of the R101 and private enterprise was preparing to produce the R100. The Air Ministry was very good to me in giving me information and sending me slides and so forth on which I could build up an interesting paper and this was while the airship was being built. The R100 was starting to be built at the same time and I didn't have details about it, but suffice it to say here that it was to be lifted by hydrogen gas and that the two main designers were, I think, Neville Shute, the author, and Barnes Wallis (the man who designed the bouncing bomb for the dam-buster raid). The airship went ahead on schedule or sooner and went through its trials satisfactorily and the airship was held doing nothing until the R101, which was delayed all through its manufacturing stage, was ready so that the two could operate at the same time and be compared.

Things seemed to go wrong from start to finish with the building of the R101. Gremlins got hopelessly into it. The major difficulty was the lift. This was provided by helium in bags filling each section of the construction of the dirigible. Now, when the airship was in flight and the weather rough, these bags rubbed against the dirigible construction and started to leak helium. When the helium in the outer envelope moved into the bows the airship would go along with the bows up in the air and *vice versa*, if the helium went into the tail, then the tail would go up in the air, and the bows would be pointing to earth. The designers resolved this by making the bags smaller for each section but then the engine power to weight ratio was too low. These were German diesel engines, MAN if I remember rightly. With less lift from the reduced volume of helium, more reliance had to be placed on the power of the engines to keep the aircraft in balance. Weight was shaved wherever possible, but the greatest amount could only come from redesign to lighten the engine and to produce a higher power to weight ratio. Eventually enough changes had been made for the airship to be considered air-worthy in time for a ceremonial flight from England to India. The great day came; the top brass, including the Air Minister himself, came on board for the trip to India. They set out and crossed the channel where it was raining and they were picking up as much water as possible from a tray on the roof because they would need as much as they could get for the latter part of the journey where the atmosphere would be hot and dry. When they were over Beauvais there was a change in the watch and a new coxswain, and the ship was out of trim and nose heavy. The coxswain could not get the nose up and the airship crashed into the hills. It exploded and burned and all, except I think three or four aircraftsmen, were killed. After what happened to the R101, the government decided to destroy the R100: it was just taken to pieces.

Now the flying boats: at the end of World War II there was an opportunity to do things that could not be put through at all easily at other times. One example would have been to have driven on the other side of the road so as to be the same as most countries in Europe. Of course, it still would have left a large part of the Southern Hemisphere driving on the other side of the road. Likewise in aviation. The idea was put forward by Air Chief Marshall Baker, Head of Coastal Command, at the end of the war. He pointed out that it would be a good idea to make a shift in travel from aeroplanes to flying boats. I think he was right. I don't think there is any capital of any country in the world which is more than 50 miles away from water. Flying boats are more comfortable and very suitable for freight and the costs of maintaining airports would be a fraction of what it takes for land aircraft. Although they are slower or have been, what is the rush? And in any case there could be land aircraft for the very small proportion of the total population who either want or specially need to travel very fast. A great opportunity missed.

My father took my brother and me up in a French aeroplane at Étaples, Pas de Calais for a circuit and bump. It took off and landed on the beach. We sat in a sort of eggshell with the pilot behind us and the propeller behind, so it pushed the aeroplane rather than drew it as with a propeller in front of the wings. We were about 7 and 9 years old then. As an undergraduate at Cambridge I paid ten bob or so to go up and experience some aerobatics, looping the loop and so on. Sir Alan Cobham moved all around Britain with his circus. Then I applied to join the Cambridge Auxilliary Air Squadron. My father signed an official paper of agreement saying that he would allow me to join and shortly thereafter I discovered that he did it most reluctantly, so I gave up the idea. I had enough to do with science and rowing.

My Physics Tutor, Dr. de Bruny, was designing an aircraft for himself which he completed a year or two after I left and it flew I believe very nicely, but he didn't take me up in it - I had gone by then anyway. I never flew in a balloon nor in an airship though I went all over the R34 which was kept in a hangar at East Fortune, just south of North Berwick. The R34, I think, flew across the North Atlantic twice. Its fate, however, like the R100, was sealed by the government with the R101 fatality.

OXFORD GROUP

It was around the mid 1930s that I became involved with the Oxford Group, as it was first called. The founder was Frank Buchman, an American. He was an unprepossessing little man and didn't even speak very well but he was genuine. He was sure the Christian Churches were on the way out, but that personal commitment to Christian values would benefit society and individuals alike. Several of my friends had been approached to join the group and some of these objected strongly to what they perceived as pressure to disclose their beliefs and join the group. When that sort of thing occurred and I knew about it, I would speak out in favour of the Group. Buchman heard about this and wanted to know who this Lubbock was. I met him in London with his people and attended several meetings. (Incidentally, Lord Salisbury was a Buchmanite.) When we had been together a little he asked me to join up with him. He felt that he had been guided to do so. I refused on the grounds that I had a life ahead of me which, in intention at least, was not unworthy and he just said, "Oh well, that's all right. You've got a great service to render in your field" and he never mentioned it again. But later on, I think at our wedding, he gave us an Egyptian tear glass. He was genuine, he didn't collect money from people and ran on a deficit mostly. The work continues all over the world, in India and Australia and everywhere. The focus of the work is still getting people to listen to God - if you listen to God, God speaks: that's the idea and it is a darn sight better than listening to the Pope.

In talking with my undergraduate friends interested in the Oxford Group, I took the line that there could be no evidence of God speaking and that it is all a matter of faith; however one might be led to do some apparently crazy things and to be adamant that they were right because of God.

I should now say what I personally believe: I believe that God is Love and I prefer to think of it the other way round - Love is God. It gets away from the view of the Deity as being anything like a human being. I believe that there is good and bad in everyone and that the only way of getting on with your enemy is to search out the good in him. Often the bad turns out to be due to bad environment and probably I would not have been able to overcome that environment if I had been in that person's shoes. (See "The Fragility of Goodness: Luck and Ethics in Greek Tragedy and Philosophy", by Martha Nussbaum).

The failure of the Churches to carry the advances of science into appropriate forms of society for the benefit of man has resulted in a break out of evangelism, some of it bogus for money-making purposes. So this line of progress is floundering. The way forward seems to me ecumenical in the widest sense, getting back to the original precepts and shaking off the present churches like some animals shed their skins.

The above is my only direct factual contact with the break away from the Churches.

JOINING UP AND TRAINING

At that time I was deeply absorbed in the work for "Food, Health and Income" and it was then that I fell in love with Minty.

When I proposed to Minty, she refused me (Minty claims I never did in fact propose to her). I thought, this is the real thing and I'm just not going to be turned off like that, so all being fair in love and war, I went to her father and I asked him to help me get her to accept me. This he quite happily agreed to do, and then the situation changed markedly. He talked to his daughter and said "I understand you and David are engaged". Minty's hair stood on end and she was absolutely appalled and then she thought that someone with as much cheek as I had might be a reasonable husband for her and she came round.

We were settling in to live at Newton when war broke out. I remember the announcement very well. The sirens going on a Sunday morning as I was motoring North in the car through Laurencekirk. People were coming out of their doors and leaning out of windows as the news was being broadcast on the radio. I made an application to fight, lodged it with the University Recruitment Board and waited. Nothing happened for a long time - I mean weeks - then I was called before the Board. One of the members of the Board got up and said to Mr. Chairman, that I had a job to fulfil at the Rowett Institute and that I should not be sent to the war. I was rather puzzled and didn't know quite what to do, but Arthur Crichton, the Head of the Duthie Experimental Farm of the Rowett was on the recruitment board and I turned to Arthur and said look, you know you could do much better without me - just put them straight and let me go to the war. Thus I joined the Royal Naval Volunteer Reserve as a trainee for the Fleet Air Arm. Weeks later I moved one stage further - I was interviewed by the Fleet Air Arm medical officer and I wanted, like everyone else, to be a pilot. They told me that my eyesight wasn't good enough and that I was to be an observer. So I think I asked them how much better a pilot's eyesight should be than an observer's eyesight - but I never really got an answer. What they wanted was people to become observers because that list was very thin and the pilot's waiting list was very high.

Eventually I was called up to St. Vincents, Gosport, to start training. There we did square bashing. And on the day of passing out from that course the external asked one of us after another to take command of the platoon and he would say what he wanted us to make them do; on this day this particular chap was terrified and external examiner asked him to get them to take off their hats for which the order in the Navy was "Remove Head-dresses". Well he scratched his head - he couldn't remember what the order was - and in despair he said "Platoon undress"!

At Portsmouth we ratings slept in the hammocks head to foot. These were slung over the mess decks, that is to say where we had our meals and some mornings I had difficulty in not vomiting, for the stench of somebody's feet on one side and the stench of somebody else's feet on the other side was pretty powerful; but it really became for me practically unbearable when the breakfast was brought in of pilchards, the smell of which I could hardly tolerate under any conditions. Correcting the page proofs of "Feeding the people in wartime" helped me and I never actually succumbed to vomiting. As a married man I could sleep out - I can't remember how many nights of the week - and Minty and I had taken a tiny little flat at the entrance to Portsmouth Harbour. That was fascinating watching the ships go through the entrance and to see the submarine base across the water. At this point Mr. Quisling, the Norwegian traitor, was active, and it seemed that Portsmouth barracks was likely to be bombed. One fat boy, Mr. Partridge, and I were held responsible for the defence. We had a rifle each and six rounds of ammunition each.

Then we went to Lee-on-Solent for our flying training. There the defences were even worse: as far as I remember the rifles were made of wood. Once, in the middle of the night, we were woken up and told that the invasion had started and we were to defend Southampton, the Isle of Wight and the area. And so we got out our loose-leaf code books and various forms of how to report which and what and were totally confused to start with. I picked up that there was a destroyer coming in at 40 knots and then there was an announcement that the invasion hadn't started at all, this was just a practice. Okay. We analysed the practice the next day. I was accused of spoiling the whole exercise. I wasn't meant to invent a cruiser coming in, a submarine there and so forth. But I thought that was what I was to do, and somebody else picks it up and saves the situation by shooting them.

The gunnery school at Portsmouth was the acme of the Portsmouth training. I remember that when the battle was engaged, and the Bismark was out, and their Lordships brought the major fighting vessels into play, they had learnt everything at the gunnery school at Portsmouth. Well we went on and they taught pilots how to fly and the observers how navigate and how to report and so forth. I was on a WT [wireless telegraphy] exercise one day - a lovely sunny day - and we flew over Wiltshire. I got through to the Ground Station and they acknowledged and told me to change wavelengths to a shorter wavelength which in those days was very difficult and I was afraid that I would fail to manage it. I worked at it like fury, taking coils out and putting other coils in and so forth and eventually I got through. A message was being sent insistently - once you are WT operator you know the emotion of the man or women who is sending you the message. So I was through and I thought that is wonderful and I sat back with sweat pouring off my brow to start taking down the message. The message was "Air raid warning red." So I looked up in the sky and there were masses of German Stukas - we got down very quickly! The switch of emotion between being so pleased at having managed the WT exercise, followed by the seriousness of the message being sent is something I shall always remember as a sort of kink in my mind I think. The Fleet Air Arm administration decided to halve our course after a certain point of our development and they split us into two groups; one group had to go to Canada to train, and the other group was to remain in the UK and train here. Well, I was in the group that was to stay. The group that went in the ship to go to Canada was torpedoed and all lives lost. Then intelligence came in to say that Lee-on-Solent was going to be bombed so they thought they would do a neat job - it had to be quick - they took us in at RAF aerodrome Ford a few miles away. That weekend they bombed Ford and they never bombed Lee. I had a stinking cold that day and had taken a nearby house because Minty's father and mother had come down to us and I wasn't fit to go for service in the aerodrome. It was a terrible slaughter but we were out of range.

I have to go back a step because Dunkirk took place when we were at Lee-on-Solent. I asked permission to go and get the Mhuc Mara to help ferry the army across the Channel. I was not granted it. We were immediately sent up to Condor. This was to be an aerodrome, but there were still JCBs and tractors clearing the ground for runways.

LETTER TO SISTER PEGGY
ABOUT BEING SHOT DOWN

Newton of Stracathro, Brechin, Angus.
Saturday, 29th September, 1990.

Darling Peg,

When I saw you last week in Lennox Gardens I was on my way back from attending a memorial service for my air gunner, David Beer, who was killed in the torpedo attack that we made on shipping in Kirkness Harbour in 1941. I am putting this on tape in case you might like to hear something of the saga.

First of all the peculiar thing is that this should have happened at all in 1990, 49 years after the event, that is after the Kirkness raid. It has popped out of the past due to Gorbachev and glasnost. By the end of the war the land on which we came down, which was then in the hands of the Germans, had changed hands and now belongs to the USSR. What had happened was by the end of the war the Russians had pushed the Germans back beyond where the remains of our aircraft lay. The area is in the Arctic Circle. The three harbours concerned are Petsamo, Murmansk and of course Kirkness, all facing towards the North Pole. The reason for the raid was as follows.

Germany, with operation Barbarossa, started to invade Russia on the 22nd of June, 1941 so Russia came into the war on our side. To help Russia we started to send convoys of equipment to Murmansk, a terribly vulnerable route, costing a lot of our shipping and hundreds of our men. Nevertheless, enough was getting through to Murmansk to worry the Germans. Our intelligence suggested that the Germans were planning to capture Murmansk and that they were amassing shipping in Kirkness harbour to transfer their ships eastward along the coast and land them east of Murmansk and attack Murmansk both from the east and the west, thus squeezing the Russians out of the harbour.

Winston Churchill wanted more operations against the German forces to demonstrate support for the new ally Stalin. Our Admiralty responded by planning to send a Task Force of two aircraft carriers with escorting war ships to torpedo shipping in Kirkness Harbour and to bomb Petsamo Harbour. The two aircraft carriers were HMS Victorious and HMS Furious. Victorious was brand new and Furious was in World War I. Originally she was a cruiser but then she was converted so that aeroplanes could fly off the deck and, incidentally, Minty's father was transferred from the army to the navy to serve on Furious in World War I. Anyway, there were two air Albacore squadrons on Victorious, numbers 827 and 828. I was in 828 Squadron. Furious had just one squadron of Albacores, No. 817, and one squadron of Swordfish, No. 812. We had fighter protection by Fairy Fulmars of 809 Squadron from Victorious, and 800 Squadron from Furious.

We set off from Scapa Flow on July 28th, 1941, I think it was, and entered Sades Fjord in Iceland to refuel. Furious did not have much tankage of fuel and had to refuel at sea on the way later from a naval fuelling ship. On the way to Iceland in the night we sailed through a mine field, said to be our own. I dare say that was malicious gossip. Anyway, one of our destroyers was hit by a mine and had its bow knocked off. It arrived the next day in Sades Ford travelling backwards. I think about a quarter of the men were killed by the mine explosion. Next day we left Iceland, heading north. As we were not going to touch land again and therefore there was no danger of a leakage of information regarding our objective, we were told what that was going to be. As I have said earlier, this was to be raids on transport shipping in Kirkness Harbour and then on the Harbour of Petsamo. 827 Squadron and 828, my Squadron, were to torpedo transport shipping in Kirkness Harbour. Since I was of the Wavy Navy, that's RNVR, the Royal Naval Volunteer Reserve, and not the regular navy, I was a little naive about the procedure for the detailed planning. I thought the right thing to do was to indicate to the higher command how our Squadron envisaged going about the job. I wrote out a plan to attack at one o'clock in the morning. The midnight sun would give us enough light but hopefully not enough for the Germans to see us clearly, and to make the attack from a high level, swooping down firing our torpedoes and getting out at sea level, making our way back to the carrier. Lieutenant Commander David Langmore, our Commanding Officer, thought my plan was good and although he was in the regular Navy, he decided to have it semaphored to the flag ship to Admiral Wake-Walker who was the Commander of the force. The only result was that David Langmore got a rocket, that is something of a reprimand, for having the effrontery to make the suggestion!

From Iceland we were heading towards Spitzbergen. Our two squadrons had to provide anti-submarine patrol for the force all the time. One aircraft at a time was enough. We flew with four depth charges attached to the underside of our wings to drop into the water over any enemy submarine we may have seen. This seldom happened, because almost invariably the submarine sees the aeroplane before the aeroplane sees the submarine, which immediately crash dives and usually gets away. HMS Furious needed to refuel before the attack to give it enough fuel for getting back to Scapa Flow after the raid. It was known to us where the refuelling ship should be but it was difficult to locate even from the air because of the Arctic fog which prevailed in masses of patches over the sea. One of our aircraft, however, was successful in finding the refuelling ship and the Furious was refuelled successfully. We carried on in the direction of Spitzbergen, but turned east and south towards Kirkness without having gone nearer than 50 miles to Spitzbergen.

Navigating was difficult near the North Pole. I dare say it is not so difficult now with the more modern equipment but we were dependent on magnetic compasses and the nearer you get to the magnetic North Pole, the more wayward your compass becomes. When flying on anti-submarine patrol for the force of carriers and destroyers you naturally fly ahead and back and forth across the path that the Force is going to go on. In Albacores, the Observer is the navigator and that of course was me in our aircraft. When you were due to return to the carrier, you gave your pilot a course to steer. At the appointed moment, if you were lucky, your pilot would see the aircraft carrier as you approached perhaps half a mile away; but then, if you were unlucky, the carrier would go into a fog bank and completely disappear. You were not allowed to communicate with your Task Force by wireless for fear that you would give away to the enemy the fact that there was a Task Force in the vicinity and by Radar they would be able to pin-point where you were. If at close quarters you lost sight of the carrier because of fog, you had a great difficulty in finding it again. We all, however, managed it successfully.

When we came within a hundred miles of Kirkness, the weather cleared, the fog was gone and there wasn't a cloud in the sky. It was just before midday. The raid was about to begin. We got our instructions from our Commander Observer on the bridge of the carrier. That was all 21 of us Observers. From there we went to our aircraft on the flight deck and climbed in, each to our own aircraft to join our pilot and air gunner. Each Albacore was loaded with one torpedo. We took off the flight deck one after the other and formed up in formation above the carrier in bright sunlight. At this point we were spotted by a German reconnaissance aircraft which simply could not have missed seeing us. The element of surprise was, of course, gone. Admiral Wake-Walker decided to carry on with the raid. We ourselves didn't know that we had been spotted but we suspected that it was inevitable that either we were already spotted or very soon would be. Having formed up in formation we headed for Kirkness Harbour and dropped down to sea level in order to try and get in under the Radar scan. Recently we have learnt from Norwegians who, as young men and adolescents were forced to work for the Germans at the Kirkness aerodrome and their headquarters, that the order was sent out to alert all the anti-aircraft batteries of a raid being imminent. The squadrons of German Messerschmitt 110s and Stuka dive bombers, all of which were in the air waiting to escort a bombing raid against Murmansk, were told to drop their bombs in a reasonably safe place and mass over Kirkness Harbour to await our arrival. The Kirkness raid was consequently a disaster. All 21 of us from 828 and 827 squadrons went into the harbour and launched our torpedoes under anti-aircraft fire and attacking enemy airplanes.

We have since learned that not one torpedo exploded. Their exploding mechanism was of a new design and was magnetic. It is said that they did not go off because there was a lot of iron ore in the rocks and hills round Kirkness: I don't believe it - I think there was a fault in the design and they would not have gone off even if there were no iron ore in the hills. Eleven Albacores out of the 21 were lost and three of the 12 Fulmars of 809 Squadron were lost. These Fairy Fulmars were our fighter protection, flying high above us to attack the aircraft that were attacking us and so limit their ability to shoot us down.

The Petsamo raid was a secondary affair but it was not the fiasco of the Kirkness raid. Three aircraft were lost, with four more damaged and seven aircrew were missing. No great damage seemed to have been done. Altogether the operation was a disaster in every respect except in Winston Churchill's objective of providing a political gesture to Stalin so most of us were the victims of a political gesture. Many of my friends lost their lives to practically no avail. I was lucky to survive. My luck all through the war was phenomenal.

The rest of this is an attempt to describe how the pilot, "Skid" Bellairs, and I were taken prisoner. We were luckier than those of us in 828 Squadron who got back to HMS Victorious. I don't really know what happened to 827 but my Squadron, 828, was posted, when they got back to Scapa Flow, to the defence of Malta. They must have done a heroic job there and to great avail because the defence of Malta was crucial to the war effort, in fact to winning the war, but every one of the air crew, pilots, observers and air gunners, were killed except one, Chief Petty Officer Smith whom I met at Lee-on-Solent last week. He and I are the sole survivors of 828 Squadron which had to be disbanded after their defence of Malta because there was nobody left.

You can imagine it came as a terrible shock to me when he told me that there were none left. Of course, some died of old age. These were ones like Skid Bellairs, my pilot, who were prisoners of war with me. The rest of the saga which follows is just what happened to us after we had fired the torpedo and turned back to return to the aircraft carrier which, of course, we were unable to do.

****

Now alas, time has slipped by, with many other things that I had to cope with and now it is many days later. Before going on with the story, you may imagine what an emotional upheaval it was for me to meet

CPO Smith of our Squadron in 1990 in Lee-on-Solent, having not seen him since the day of the raid in July, 1941. I think it was much the same for him.

****

Well now, to carry on with the saga....

Having flown into Kirkness Harbour and having let our torpedo off and run, we turned and headed to get out of the harbour, hugging the rocks of the foreshore as close as possible to make it more difficult for the anti-aircraft fire and for an attacking aircraft to get in a sustained burst of fire at us. We were followed out by our sister Albacore, piloted by McKie, a great friend of mine, and the Observer Paton, who incidentally was a friend of Laura Grimmond's, and their air gunner, Corner. They were caught by a German Messerschmitt 110 fighter aircraft. The Albacore crashed onto the rocks and burst into flames. None survived but I hope they were all three killed outright. This same enemy aircraft caught us up and opened fire on us. We were still flying just above the rocks and there was no room for us to turn to get out of the line of fire. Our air gunner, Jan Beer, managed to get a good burst of fire with our machine gun at the enemy Messerschmitt 110 before we were hit by its canon shells. Jan was hit through the throat, spun round into my arms, dead. Mercifully it was instantaneous although blood spurted all over me. The rear gun was destroyed; we lost the outer part of our starboard wing; my pilot, Skid Bellairs, was fortunately untouched but I was lightly showered with metal splinters. Unluckily one nicked the supraorbital artery which naturally proceeded to spurt more blood and the drop in blood pressure in the eyes caused me first to lose colour vision - I could only see in black and white - and then I went completely blind and could not see. I put a finger on the puncture of the artery to stem the loss of blood, but not hard enough to prevent a loss of flow to the eyes. It was touch and go. It worked and gradually my eyesight returned, although I had to keep my finger on the artery. When I began to see again, the Messerschmitt 110 had disappeared, possibly shot down by Jan, but another German fighter which I took to be a Messerschmitt 109, but it was probably a Stuka, according to recent information, was approaching us and firing at us. By this time we were over water. I called to Skid through the communication tube to turn and we were scarcely hit. Our port wing, however, on turning, just dipped into the sea - or rather it is better to say "tipped" as it only just touched and Skid, who was a superb pilot, managed to pull up and straighten out and carry on towards the aircraft carrier, Victorious.

At this point Skid told me that he did not have enough wing surface to be able to land on the carrier so, according to my contingency instructions given to me by my Commander Observer on the carrier before we took off, I gave Skid an easterly course to head for Russia, the USSR. Thus we came back over land, still being attacked by this enemy, single-engined fighter aircraft. With but a single front machine gun, which is all an Albacore has, and which Skid was only once in a position to use and then only for a second, virtually our only course of action was to defend ourselves by turning in a tighter circle than our attacker could. I have to explain that in an Albacore the pilot in a cockpit has the large petrol tank filling the whole of the width and height of the fuselage behind him and the observer and air gunner are further behind the petrol tank, so in order to time our turns, I had to tell Skid when to make the turn by speaking through what we called the Gosport tube. It is just like the tube that houses used to have in our youth where you blew down it to the kitchen below the ground and communicated with the cook or chef as to what you wanted. From here on flying east towards the USSR overland, we continued our dogfight with the enemy aircraft coming up behind us and I waiting until he started firing and then calling on Skid to turn. The tricky part was when to tell him to turn. If I called on him to turn too soon then the pilot of the enemy aircraft could follow us round and get our aircraft into his firing sights. If I called too late, he would have been able to shoot us down by getting too many bullets into our aeroplane before we turned. I found in practice that it was necessary to let him just start hitting us before turning, otherwise he could follow us round.

While this was going on Skid called back to me to say that there was an Albacore coming towards us in the opposite direction, flying west and it was being attacked by an enemy aircraft. He thought they were getting shot up badly so when they were about to pass us, really quite close, we waved like mad to encourage them in their fight.

I have to break off now to tell you of something that happened after the war in relation to this. Immediately after the war, before being demobilised, the Navy gave me a medical check-up. For part of this I had to go to the Naval eye specialist place just at the south end of the Forth Bridge. After the examination there I went in my car to cross the Forth by the ferry - that was the way to go before the Forth Road Bridge was built. While waiting for the ferry on the jetty, I saw another naval officer standing about on foot, so I went up and asked him if I could give him a lift and I thought I recognised his face slightly. He accepted my offer; he was going to Donnybristle aerodrome which was just on the north side of the Forth in Fife. Naturally we got talking. It appeared that he had been on the Kirkness/Petsamo raid. We had been attacking Kirkness and he had been attacking Petsamo. He belonged to 827 Squadron, the sister Squadron to ours, the 828, both of which were on the Victorious. He then began to tell me that an extraordinary thing had happened to them. After they had raided Petsamo they had been attacked by enemy aircraft and were flying west when they came across another Albacore being attacked heavily flying east. I said to him, don't tell me any more - they waved to you! He said yes, the bloody fools, they waved to us. Anyway it must have encouraged them or done them good, because they got back to the aircraft carrier and we didn't! The officer's name, incidentally, was Lieutenant Ball.

To get back to the story. We went on being attacked, turning and being attacked and turning again, as far as I can remember, about 15 times. Gradually more bits were falling off our aircraft. I remember at one point Skid called me up to say that his air speed indicator had flown out of the window. It ended with the enemy aircraft running out of ammunition - he just flew alongside and took a look at us and all would have been well except that Skid said he could not keep the aeroplane in the air any longer. He made an absolutely superb landing in the Tundra, with even the undercarriage and wheels still intact. I congratulated Skid on the landing he made and the piloting of the aircraft altogether, it was simply wonderful. About the landing he said the ground was very good for this kind of difficulty but we had a lot of holes in the fuselage and the wings, although the engine held out extremely well. The last time we made a tight turn, so little of the controls were left that Skid could hardly get it back onto an even keel - we flew round twice tighter before he could do so. Anyway the Tundra where we landed was flat country with scrub trees three or four feet high.

Now I must divert again to talk about Skid. His eyesight was bad and he had lenses fitted into his goggles. How he got the Navy to take him on as a pilot, I really don't know, but he was a man of great determination, partly because of this probably. Although he was a superb pilot, he was a hopeless navigator. He was a rich lad who, I believe, owned a large part of the Miles Aircraft Company. Miles Magister was a very well known aircraft before the war. He used to fly his own Miles aircraft for his own private use. He would fly over to Le Touquet and gamble and come back. He was then all right, but when he was flying over land he didn't know, he used to get hopelessly lost so he would fly until he had no petrol left and, having got himself thoroughly lost, he would make a forced landing! So he was very experienced in making forced landings and landing in the Tundra was no great difficulty for him, despite the fact that the aircraft was extremely difficult to fly after having lost so much of it by being shot at so many times.

We left my air gunner, Jan Beer's body in the fuselage of the aircraft as being the best we could do having no reasonable means of burying him. Skid and I started walking east to try to get through the German lines to the Russian lines. I was weak from loss of blood and I had three metal splinters sticking slightly out of the eye which prevented me from blinking. I could either have the eyelid permanently up or permanently down by pulling it. I think I was having some hallucinations for I thought I saw a building half a mile away on the right and I asked Skip to go and see if there was anyone there. It turned out that there was no building and nothing there; in fact there were no people or buildings around us for miles. Stumbling along through the Tundra I fell and to my delight found ground cover of blueberries. Being perhaps extra thirsty through lack of blood, I was delighted and we gathered them and consumed as many as we could. Skid had come through the whole adventure physically unscathed and was a great support to me. Towards midnight we lay down to try to sleep under the midnight sun. It was surprisingly cold, having been very hot through the day. The next day we walked on until we came to a large stream or burn and I decided to walk down it towards the sea, for I thought we were bound to come across people before we got to the coast who might be civilians, either Finns or possibly Norwegians.

When we got to where the burn had widened into a small river we did find a civilian who was fishing. This was near to the German line. I asked him for help in the little German that I had, having no Finnish or Norwegian. He packed up his fishing rod and indicated for us to follow him. Our hopes were at first very high but then we began to suspect that instead of trying to help us he was about to take us into the German line. This unfortunately was so and we became prisoners of war - inevitably, because we were both pretty well exhausted and I was incapable of running.

Incidentally, just recently we have been told by Norwegians who were about there that it was a Finn who gave us up. Maybe we were too close to the Germans anyway. We were taken into a makeshift wooden hut where we were to be interrogated. An army major, the Hauptmann, started to interrogate Skid while a young army medical officer came to look at my eye. He was an extremely nice lad who had obviously taken the Hippocratic Oath seriously. There was a table and two stools in this part of the hut. He sat me down on one stool and sat on the other himself. He froze my eye and started to dig the splinters out with a scalpel. One of the three proved difficult to get out. "Es ist so tief" he kept murmuring. Sweat poured down his face. Meanwhile, in the other part of the hut, I heard much German shouting. I asked the doctor to go through and see what was happening. Clearly I could hear that the Hauptmann was shouting abuse at Skid. The doctor came back to say he was worried for the life of my pilot. Skid was dark complexioned with a prominent nose and curly, ebony black hair and the Hauptmann took him for a German Jew who had defected to the allied side. Well, I had been talking with the doctor through bad German on my side and bad English on his, but both being biologists, we had quite a lot of scientific common ground. I told the doctor that Skid was not a Jew but that he was a Cornishman and that as he, the doctor, would know, much of the Cornish human stock came from the Iberian peninsular and that the people were not Jews but had that swarthy appearance. Fortunately for Skid he had no German whatsoever and the Hauptmann swearing at him caused very little effect - he just smiled benignly back at the Hauptmann: I would love to have seen it. Anyway the doctor went back and persuaded the interrogator that Skid was not a Jew but a Cornishman and the noise of shouting and swearing eased down. The lad finished treating my eye and said that when I got to wherever they were going to take us, I should insist on having a doctor look at the eye again. This lad no doubt saved my eyesight and also probably saved Skid's life. I wish I had been able to trace him after the war, although it is more than likely that he would not have survived.

Skid and I were taken back to Kirkness in a Red Cross truck. I think most of the regular troops were moved back and forth in trucks marked with the Red Cross. Not that the Russians would have paid much attention to that! We spent the night at Kirkness. I asked to see a doctor for my eye but the following morning I was taken to an aeroplane and flown south to Oslo. Skid was left behind and so we had to part. Once again I was terribly worried that they would do away with Skid. In the aeroplane I decided that the sooner I could attempt to escape, the easier it would be so I intended to make a run for it at Oslo aerodrome. We got out of the aeroplane into what felt to me stiflingly hot air and before I could get moving at all, I fainted. So much for my first attempt at escape!

I was taken by a German Luftwaffe officer in a car from the aerodrome to Oslo gaol. The officer had a stiff leg due to a wound he had received while piloting a bomber aircraft over Aberdeen some months earlier. I sat in the back of the car with an officer sticking a revolver into my ribs. On the way a Norwegian car came towards us and practically blocked the road ahead. I think they knew I was a prisoner and were making a possible opportunity for me to escape, but a) I was too weak, and b) I would have received a bullet from the revolver unless I had been very clever. I spent the weekend in Oslo gaol. I got a doctor to see my eye on the Sunday, a German doctor of course, and he was really angry at having to come and look at a prisoner's wound. He took one look and said I was all right and went off. He did nothing to treat it. In the prison I was asked who was our best fighter ace in the RAF. I said that we did not have "aces" like they did in the Luftwaffe. They wanted to crow over me about Douglas Bader being brought down and were disappointed that I hadn't mentioned him. When they told me I replied that if all they could do was to shoot down pilots with no legs, they weren't much good! One had to keep up one's morale. It was terribly hot in the prison - it was the first week of August, 1941. Much of the inside of the building was made of heavy wood, beams and so forth. It was somewhat claustrophobic and I wondered what it would be like if a fire started. The worst of it was a prisoner in the cell above mine, whose footsteps I could here walking back and forth on the few feet that he had for hours on end. I know that if I had a choice between capital punishment and life imprisonment, I would choose to be killed. On the Monday I had the ignominy of being taken in a troop train of Germans through neutral Sweden, believe it or not, and across into Denmark and south into Germany to Frankfurt am Main where the Germans had their Luftwaffe transit camp. On the way through Sweden, when we stopped at a station, I tried to get out - and did get out of the train - but couldn't get away from the German troops. The Germans were not hard on me, they were not wanting to show bad behaviour in front of the Swedes and when we got going again they had quietened down.

One of my two guards was a nice fellow who had been an opera singer. He was obviously not a Nazi. He told me "You are my good luck" - what he meant was that this was giving him a break: by taking me into Germany he was being given some leave and could go and see his family. He wrote to me after the war but we lost contact when I went to America.

About a couple of days after I was in the transit camp, Douglas Bader turned up, also on his own. We had both fallen into enemy hands on the same day. I had not known him before meeting up in Germany. However, we started trying to make a tunnel from the transit camp which was a very feeble amateurish attempt, but we continued in the same vein so long as we were together, first in Lubeck, then in Warburg and then Stalag Luft III. But after a time they took Douglas to Colditz and sent me as far away as possible in the opposite direction to a camp in Poland. It was not until we were in Stalag Luft III in Upper Silesia, a place called Sagan, that Skid Bellairs, my pilot, caught up with me. To my very great relief nothing seriously untoward had happened to him in the intervening time.

After the war I went to America to help to start up the Food and Agriculture Organisation, that is to help my father in law who became the first Director General. I lost contact with Skid. He died a natural death about two years ago, I believe. I had started a new phase of life and I didn't want to think about war time at all, and Minty didn't want to hear about any of it anyway - it made her too sad. Her brother, Billy, was killed when a rear gunner in an aircraft of Coastal Command in the Channel. I didn't want to read books about the war; I didn't want to see films about the war; I bottled up the whole of that phase of my life and sealed it off, so to speak.

Now, suddenly, with Gorbachev's glasnost allowing the Norwegians to collect the remains of the aircraft in which we were brought down, the whole saga has opened up. Telling it to you has been a sort of catharsis for me. I am afraid it may either be very dull to you, or distressing and it is a strange 91st birthday present to you - or is it only the 90th? But here it is anyway.

With all my love,
Brother David.[4]

I don't suppose my experiences are so very different from everyone else's - the main difference is that I survived the war. My colleagues of 828 Squadron were all killed, thanks I believe to high level Admiralty not knowing how to use the Fleet Air Arm. It was a wonderful service which, if it had been understood by their Lordships of the Admiralty, would have shortened the war and lowered the expense - one cannot say more. When practically all of our battle wagons had been sunk, perhaps more attention started to be paid, but it was too late.

****

---

[4]   **Notes for the Kirkness story:**
a). Jan may have got a shot into the 110. It takes very little to upset that aeroplane and maybe that is why it turned away and did not continue to attack us. On the other hand, it probably would not be prepared to go far out over the sea because of shortage of fuel.
Although the encounter with the 110 was tragic it might be said that with the 109 honours were even for about the time when Skid said he couldn't keep the aeroplane in the air any longer, the 109 came up alongside and did not shoot, presumably because he had run out of ammunition.
b). Birth of Ann Pat 12 days later. News of birth came through Andrew Bigger in POW camp. First communication from the Admiralty as they didn't know whether I was alive or dead, would my wife please return £40 of her living allowance.

Dictated in 1991 for <u>Stalag Luft III</u> being written by Charles Rollings

August 1941 Dulag Luft. It happened that Group Captain Douglas Bader and I fell into enemy hands on the same day, he at St Omer in north France and I in the Arctic Circle. We met up for the first time in the Dulag where, since I had a degree in natural sciences and was likely to be the nearest to a medical doctor that he would come across, he asked me to stay with him to help him look after his legs. With one Flt. Lt. Peter Gardner we naively started to tunnel from the hut we were in, were discovered in short order and were sent with a draft of about twenty to a camp just outside Lübeck.

End August 1941 Lübeck. The commandant was a Nazi army officer who spoke of "guns, not butter." We had no Red Cross parcels nor letters from home. The clever camp cat, eventually caught with difficulty in his ninth life, was consigned to the pot. We did not have enough time to make an attempt to escape here as the Dulag contingent was soon moved thence to Warburg.

September 1941 Warburg. Here to our joy we met practically all the British army officer PoWs of that time including of course many friends. An erstwhile colleague of mine from the Rowett Institute sought me out to congratulate me on being the father of a daughter and that mother and child were well. The best news I ever had! While waiting in transit for Stalag Luft III, the Luftwaffe "escape proof" camp, to be made ready for us, four of us temporarily escaped. We were helped by Major David Maud, who faked the count of a posse on a visit to the clothing store outside the perimeter wires. It was in the winter snow. Smith got away but was caught a few days later, not having been able to contact help. Pete Gardner, Bader and I were immediately picked up by a chance soldier on his way back from the latrines. In the guard-house an N.C.O. banged down the butt of his rifle with bone-breaking force on the foot of one of us. He gaped with amazement when the blow was received with equanimity. It was Douglas's! In the Spring of 1942 we were moved by train to Sagan to start life in Stalag Luft III. On the way we had a protracted stop in one station. An engine drew up outside our window on the next line…

We had managed at Warburg to gain possession of a tea-pot and were looking at it to see that it was still unbroken. The engine driver leaned out of his cabin and indicated that he would fill it with boiling water for us; so we handed it over only to see the engine immediately disappear. We not only cursed the German race but also ourselves for having been conned. However the engine appeared back 5 minutes later and the driver, *mirabile dictu*, handed us over a steaming pot of tea!

****

HOW I WAS PLACED IN
STALAG LUFT III

We came from Oflag 6B which was essentially an army officers' camp where we had been waiting until Stalag Luft III had been completed as an escape-proof camp. Flight Lieutenant Pete Gardiner and I were with Wing Commander Douglas Bader. I because having some qualifications in physiology and biochemistry could possibly help him with his legs. There was only one prisoner doctor in the camp, and he was a gynaecologist. We lived and messed in a privileged, 3-bunk end of a big wooden hut and Douglas had a batman so we were well off and in those circumstances not really knowing quite so much about the life of the camp as if I had been in the centre of a hut with 15 or so others. However, they sent Bader to Colditz and a contingent in which I was placed in the opposite direction to Schubin in Poland. The contingent in Poland came back to Stalag Luft III and there I joined Aidan Crawley and friends in a 15 bunk room. Much of our time was taken up in escape committee matters, but we managed to take part in other activities. Charlie Hopetown, an heir to Linlithgo and others wrote a play, a skit or burlesque with music and dancing which was good. The working up of it and the rehearsals as well as the performances which everyone seemed to enjoy were good occupation. We had a music group and we sang parts of The Messiah and various classical music as well as jazz.

At the start of the escape through the wooden horse we were singing in the hut from which the horse was to be carried out and this sound was partly a diversion to keep the Germans from becoming interested. I remember we were singing the part "And He shall give his angels charge over thee lest thou dash thy foot against a stone". There is a tail piece to that: one of the wooden horse lads who got home afterwards went to Somerset to visit the home of one of the other boys; he was shown his colleague's bedroom, as it was when he was a child. Over the boy's bed was the same quotation! Alas, however, he went out to Malaysia after World War II was over and was killed in an ambush in the jungle.

With the help of the Swiss Red Cross I managed to set up a little library and to the few who were thinking of taking a medical degree or were interested in the natural sciences, I used to give a series of lectures, mainly on nutrition. There was a wealth of expertise, technical and academic, in the camp. [5]

The story of the march out of Stalag Luft III at the end has been written up extremely well by Aidan Crawley.

---

[5] **Reminder Notes:**
Wing Commander Maw and the clock. Making radio sets. Bribery. Washing facilities, defecating. Horse-drawn shit tanks. Race for horses' droppings on the so-called gardens. Walking around the perimeter. Letters. Red Cross parcels. Letter forms. Photographs in envelopes. Censuring of correspondence generally. Private parcels. Russian adjacent camps: getting them a guitar and them playing to us. Whirlwind taking all washing high up into the sky and gone for ever. "For you the war is over". Eating grass. Question of hormonal balance in sex organs without any females. Was there something as was imagined in the German food/ soup to keep down sexual desire or not?

PRE WORLD WAR II PEOPLE THAT I KNEW - WHICH MAY BE OF INTEREST: PRIME MINISTERS

Not much to it, really, but it is interesting to know the man at the top. The earliest was A.J. Balfour who lived at Whittinghame in East Lothian, not so far away. Then Herbert Henry Asquith of whom we saw quite a lot because Margot liked coming to stay with us. Baldwin I knew more about than knew, because Tommy Crathorne, Dugdale that was, was his Parliamentary Private Secretary for quite a long time. One could describe him as small and portly. I remember at one Henley Regatta I was asked down to the Hambledon's house which is just at one end of the river of the Regatta area - lovely place. I had lunch there and the Baldwins were there and as we were coming back in the launch for the afternoon session, Mrs. Baldwin, who was rather stupid I think - I don't know - anyway she piped up so that everyone should hear it: "Stanley, Stanley, I'm going to have sixpence on Jesus". I don't really know anything about her, and that may be rather unkind.

MacMillan I knew a little of, mostly on the business side because we got him to publish "Food, Health and Income". I used to go and see him in his office and discuss certain things with him about the book. MacMillan was a contemporary of Walter Elliott and the two of them, and two or three others, were in coterie of political interest more advanced than the other Conservatives. MacMillan had become a Member of Parliament, and in his constituency in the North East of England he saw the pitiful state of the working people and the unemployed in that area and he never forgot that and of course he was quite keen therefore about publishing

"Food, Health and Income" as it squared his conscience a bit. (Though probably not!)

Alec Douglas Home I knew slightly, but I knew one of his brothers who was a contemporary of mine at Eton and very, very funny. He married the daughter of the Headmaster of Eton at that time, C.A. Ellington. One got to know the daughters of the headmasters of the schools one was in to some degree. She is a very, very nice woman and Ellington's wife was a very, very nice woman too who was a Littleton before she was married. When I got into 6th Form Ellington seemed to build up an interest in me, rather greater than the rest of 6th formers. I never understood why or how it came about, but it did.

Harold Wilson I knew - but the less said about him the better. He was a traitor to Popeye, of course, and in a slimy way.

When the King got an inflamed appendix, the King's physician, Lord Dawson of Penn was naturally brought in. However, with typical Cockney humour I think, it was said that "Lord Dawson of Penn has killed so many men, that's why we sing 'God save the King'".

His son, the successor, Edward, Prince of Wales, I came across twice. Once on an Eton OTC parade on the field. He stood us at ease and gave us a short talk and early on in the short talk he said he was "particularly gratified to see ....." and then he had to look at the notes he was holding behind his back, to see what he was particularly gratified over! The other occasion was on the golf course at Muirfield when the Open was being played. In those days, of course, there were few people and they were allowed all over the course. You could follow Bobbie Jones or Walter Hagen or whoever it was that you were interested in and often you would see the putting on one green and then you would run off to the next tee, usually on an upgrade place. Well, the Prince of Wales was there incognito and I was very keen to see the next drive and I dashed off; in the scrimmage I knocked somebody over and I was horrified to find that I had knocked over the Prince of Wales! However, he didn't want to be known - he was incognito and somehow I sensed this and kept quiet. I said I am sorry and he said, I am sorry, it was my fault and he slipped off.

STRANDS EMANATING
FROM CAMBRIDGE 1930

We had Communism with science as its God. Lenin made as certain as he could that not a hair of Pavlov's head was to be touched, although he was Royalist to the end of his days. Then we had religion with the thought that, since the churches were out of touch, if there was anything in religion the way to find out was to be in touch with the Deity in one form or another. Thirdly with the feeling that the world was getting smaller, we had the belief that nations of the world must co-operate on a global basis if the objective of World War I being the war to end all wars was ever to come to fruition. There were side-shows which nevertheless were entered into wholeheartedly. Such was the Spanish Civil War. Some of my Cambridge friends fought in Franco's army and some fought on the Republican side. Numbers of them were killed there. Apart from the fact that the Germans learned a lot there about how to use their Luftwaffe in warfare, the Spanish Civil War was contained in Spain. Not so Italy and the Abyssinian war, nor Hitler's preparations for World War II.

By the Abyssinian war [1935-36], the League of Nations was tested and found wanting. The League's decision was to apply sanctions. Here oil was the most powerful lever. The best efforts of the Secretariat of the League were unable to prevent countries from cheating and getting oil into Abyssinia. I do not know of any participation of any of my friends in the Abyssinian war but I was in Geneva at the beginning of the introduction of nutrition into the League while the war was going on. Anthony Eden and Lord Halifax were out there. Eden was the Minister of Foreign Affairs. Lord Astor took me to lunch with Eden once or twice and we had discussions. Eden was at a loss as to know what to do and feeling, probably rightly, that he couldn't do anything. This is an example of the problem that we are up against with the strengthening of the United Nations in the 1992 Crux. It seems that there must be some sort of veto against countries who have agreed to uphold a United Nations objective but who are reneging in a way that damages this objective.

I don't know anything about the war of the Chinese in Mongolia: in the long run history may prove this to have been most important of all but at the time it just seemed too far away and the British and Europe as a whole were, I think, just spectators.

An equally bloody struggle, although it was not a war, was taking place in Germany. There was a division of opinion of the German people into two almost equal parts: Communism or Fascism. Britain already had a Fascist group under Oswald Moseley, who was married to one of the Mitford sisters. They and much of the British establishment were in favour of Hitler and another Mitford sister went over to see Hitler personally. I had no direct experience of the German situation except once or twice being in Germany and finding that the ordinary people, or the above average intelligence people, who were fairly well informed, under-estimated Hitler greatly.

The League of Nations was coping badly except for our introduction of nutrition and the majority of the people were in favour of the League of Nations putting its back into such a worthwhile objective.

Guy Burgess

There was a divine/ethical discontent at Cambridge in and around 1930 when for twelve years or so after World War I, the "war to end wars", the objective was not being approached by governments let alone achieved. Consequently undergraduates and graduates were seeking ways and means of advancing. There seemed to me to be three main lines being pursued, each different: Communism, Religion, and Co-operation of nations for a better world.

Screeds have been written on the subject, the importance of which dwindles as relevant historical events emerge with time. First, the defection to the USSR was immediately dubbed as traitorous. Now, since glasnost, if it is not forgotten, it may be looked upon as a reaction of two members of an F.O. defecting to help bridge the gap between UK & USSR.

I knew Guy Burgess from the time he first went to a public school and his life story is not without interest in the initiation of change in custom thought between the wars.

He came to Eton to my tutor's, F.W. Dobbs, the same half (term) as I did. Next half he didn't come back. He was sent to Dartmouth College to join the navy, his late father having been a Captain expressing in his will his anxiety to have his eldest son follow in his footsteps.

This didn't work out so FWD took him back. He was brilliant, winning top history prizes. He produced superb cartoons and other pen & ink sketches. His most famous was of an Eton "ancient light" by the name of Broadbent, who used to ask scholars and teachers out to tea for that same day. If they said they couldn't, he would say "Come Monday", "Come Tuesday", etc. till you had to accept some time. He was a cripple with a bowed back. Guy's sketch consisted of, I think, three lines and was the very live image of him. It became one of my tutor's cherished possessions. Another cartoon was "War Guilt" - a drunk supporting himself against a lamp-post. This was the first indication I saw of the reaction against the complacency of the Establishment. He and I enjoyed each other's company, I because he was a great raconteur and mimic but most because he had an unorthodox mind constantly jolted out of custom thought by strong emotions and a warm heart. Yes, a warm heart. He was intrigued by me because he couldn't understand me. Though he reckoned I was not clever, I astonished him by periodically coming out with a philosophical understanding of a situation which had not occurred to him.

I gave him his House Colours. He dribbled the ball well. He walked with his head a little down and with a slight bounce, toes turned in.

The first year I had the Mhuc Mara (my father had brought it from Tarbert, Mull of Kintyre but had become ill with a duodenal ulcer), I asked him up to stay at Glendaruel where my father had taken a grouse moor for the season to teach me to sail and handle his boat. We motored north from Birch Hall. On the way we passed Molly Grey, also motoring north. Shortly thereafter the Chrysler boiled. Molly caught us up so I introduced them. The trouble was due to a leak in the radiator. There was a field of wheat. Guy jumped the fence, picked a head and we got one or two grains into the radiator. We filled up the radiator - one grain stuck in the leak and swelled - all was well. Quite practical and somehow unexpected.

61

We reached the Kyles of Bute and there Guy taught me all he knew from his Dartmouth training about sailing. My Mother had sent over her housemaid from North Berwick to look after us. She was a very good Highlander and had a very marked Highland Gaelic accent which intrigued Guy who, a mimic by inclination, was always trying to copy behind her back. She resented this. I could not stop him; he thought she should not have minded. I was so embarrassed that if I could have sent him home I would have. As it was, I shortened our stay.

At Cambridge we seldom met. My world was science and rowing. His was History and Communism. He was an openly avowed Communist. Before he took his degree he came and told me that he was giving up the Communist party because he felt the end did not justify the means. It might have been a lie to put me (us) off the scent but then I wasn't after him.

He looked upon me as his mentor. Missed his father badly. He felt I had some good in me which he didn't understand - a mystery.

Why did Guy defect?

Later, in Washington DC, by chance at one of the diplomatic drinks parties with which we were plagued, I came across one Peter Stevens from the UK Embassy. He had been a friend of brother Peter's and mine when we were all three at private school Naish House. He told me that Guy was on the Embassy Staff. So I wrote to him but got no reply. After about 10 days I wrote again asking him to drop into my office. I must have repeated writing about another twice before one day he turned up. This was at the time of Algernon Hiss and Whittaker Chambers and a document buried in the garden in a pumpkin - a cloak and dagger business.

He didn't want to meet. However, once he had decided that I wouldn't give up, he came along. We got back onto the old footing, after I told him that I thought much of the confrontation between the UK and the USSR was due to failure to understand each other's background. From an international Civil Servant's viewpoint, I could see how stupid the FO's reactions often were and how stupid the Kremlin's often were (I can't remember hard facts and instances here, alas). I said that the people of the Soviets would not settle down with the Chinese because they looked upon the "Chinks" as inferior people, but their inclination was rather towards the White Western Civilisation and that is the way the chips would eventually fall.

I got Guy to come to our house in Friendship Heights once or twice. He loved playing with our children and strumming on the piano. One day in 1951 when we were to return home, the day before Ann Pat, Minty and I started to motor over to the West Coast, he came to say goodbye. As he played the piano, beads of sweat started to form on his face. Someone came to pick him up, I think it was MacLean's wife as he was staying with them in the house that had belonged to Alger Hiss (wheels within wheels). She said to me, as Guy introduced us, "Oh, does Guy guide your life as he does everyone else's?" Guy stopped in his tracks and said "No, its the other way round".

When we got back from our excursion to San Francisco (we sold the Cadillac there and flew back to Washington) we were organising our goodbye party for D.C. friends including Peter Stevens who said "By the way, I suppose you know Guy Burgess has gone!" He was off, it transpired, to make his clandestine moves to slide incognito into the USSR with MacLean.

He was not a traitor. I was his mentor - I ought to know. Perhaps if he had been, the Kremlin would not have treated him so shabbily. He was one grain of mustard seed which eventually blossomed into Glasnost. (I begin to feel like R.V. Jones who appeared to believe he won the war single-handed. Look what you've done!)

ARRIVAL AT THE ROWETT

Popeye didn't want to take me on, but as Walter Elliot had suggested it he did. I had a degree in Physics, Chemistry, Physiology and Biochemistry. Popeye put me to work with John Duckworth in pure science, studying the movement of salts through semi-permeable membranes. I was 21 years old. John Duckworth realised I was a good lab technician, in other words he could rely on my work. When he heard I was going to be moved on to other areas of physiology and rushed to stop me, Popeye realised I <u>was</u> really a scientist. So Popeye did want to move me around in order for me to get experience. I went to work with Richard Garry, head of Physiology, and later Professor at Glasgow, for the study of gut, through rats.

About two years later there came a shift to a new emphasis on human nutrition. Suddenly one day Popeye said he'd been in London seeing people in the Ministry of Health and meeting Lord Linlithrow, head of the Market Supply Committee. The discussion was about how we didn't know enough about variations in food consumption, not only from the marketing side but also from health value of nutritional intake. Popeye had said it at the end of the day before taking the night train to London. I thought, "This is my line – just what I would like to get on to – a shift on to the practical side."

I talked to Nannima about it. She said Popeye was going to be down south on this for some days. I told her I thought it was time for me to go from 'rats to humans.' I asked her, "Do you think I should do it?" Nannima said she didn't know. I booked a sleeper to London. I met Popeye in the street outside his club going for tobacco. Popeye, most surprised to see me, threw up his arms and said "What's wrong?" I said I wanted to work on this new aspect of things. Popeye leaped at it. (Popeye never told anybody to do anything, he just spun a web over people and they either took something up or not. "The best work people will do is work for which they are not paid.") Popeye tried to pay me – but I wouldn't take it.

I still had a science program using rats. I was working on the histology of the rat to provide a histological standard of *mus norvegicus*. I reprogrammed it so I could do it at the weekend and work in London during the week. It was the hardest work I have ever done.

Popeye took me round the places with which they would be working – the Ministry of Health, Dr. H.E. Magee, who had been in Garry's place at Rowett. Magee gave us a lot of help opening doors for starting surveys in the East End of London and all over the U.K., and took me to the London County Council.

Popeye had by this time been made a Fellow of the Royal Society, and Lord Linlithgow was prepared to put his men to work on this project. Linlithgow gave me an office and Popeye gave me an assistant. I was working with the Market Supply Committee, consisting of 8 or 10 people in that secretariat. E.M.H Lloyd was head of the secretariat of the Market Supply Commission Committee. In a meeting with Popeye, Magee and me, they agreed to collect all the information from the surveys gathered in the past 4 years on income, food and so on. The question was how to deal with this information (see Food Health and Income on how this all was done).

Magee agreed to get what survey information there was through the Ministry of Health. A key aspect was that Lloyd got hold of a young statistician at Cambridge to devise a statistical format by dividing the U.K. income per head into 6 groups.

So I changed from being an employee at the Rowett to being Boyd Orr's assistant or representative in charge of the survey.

FOOD HEALTH AND INCOME

The great breakthrough was having the statistician breaking up the survey into 6 income groups. Faced with the difficulty of how to relate food consumption to different sections of the population, it didn't seem possible until the statistician said it could be done. Then we got Hollerith tabulating machines to get the data in. Up until then people had only done small regional surveys. It had seemed too big and impossible to do.

Data was taken from London up to the Rowett and worked on there, including by Dr. Leach (of the Imperial Bureau). It is too much to say that she was the architect of the publication, but she played a major part. Drafts were sent to Walter Elliot to keep him up with it and because he was going to have to deal with it in the House of Commons when it was published.

All these people had one objective "to show how many people were below the poverty line of requirements."

I wanted to show the relationship of heights and weights of children and adults. I got Bob Weatherall, who was science master at Eton, to measure the heights and weights of all at Eton, and that is the line of well-to-do that appears in the book.

We all knew that the book would cause a great furor so Walter Elliot lent us Harwood until it died down. The issue was taken up in Parliament and people on both sides of the house could be seen waving the book. It changed the way people in government, and people in general, thought about the situation.

I took Food Health and Income to the League of Nations and explained it to them. This introduced nutrition into international affairs. Lord Bruce, with whom we got linked up through Frank McDougall, an Australian/Scot, and Lord De La Warr introduced the debate on health in the next session of the League of Nations. After Bruce's speech and the passing of the Assembly Resolution, McDougall sent a triumphant telegram, to Boyd Orr, it parodied the words of Hugh Latimer: 'Brother Orr, we have lighted such a candle, by God's Grace, as we trust shall never be put out.' The result was a division into two groups out of which came – "Marriage of Health and Agriculture" from a committee of Economists, Agronomists and Medicos and "The Physiological Bases of Nutrition," the outcome of a high-level meeting of world Physiologists, including E.V. McColum, from the U.S., although the U.S. was not a member of League of Nations.

Long before we finished <u>Food Health and Income</u> we knew the statistical basis was thin. So we were very careful not to claim more than could be substantiated and the government statisticians said it was okay. The Carnegie Survey was a refinement of Food Health and Income to get better statistics.

BOYD ORR AT THE ROWETT

When he was getting going, he would meet with his governing body and he would charm them along very carefully chosen steps. One day Mr. Muirison said "Dr. Orr has his fist closed and he just shows us finger by finger by finger what he wants to do - where will it end?" He was, of course, a great supporter of Dr. Orr.

When Boyd Orr went over to America to discuss things with Sherman and the wrong figure for requirements got into the literature, the Rowett spotted it and had to point it out to the Americans who accepted the Rowett's logic. When he was leaving they said "I expect you will be on to calcium next", and he said, "How did you know that? I haven't spoken a word about that; I am thinking of it and I have just started". "Oh", they said, "we are watching you very closely. We admire your work". A recognised prophet, but not in his own country of Britain. He was dubbed by Beaverbrook in his newspapers *The Daily Express* and so forth as the prophet of doom. Doom of course, is the alternative if nothing is done. He knew Beaverbrook very well from his early upbringing, his religion. Beaverbrook tried his old trick on him of putting a blank cheque in front of him and saying write out any sum you like and come and join me on *The Express*. He made a big mistake there. Anyway, controversy helped bring nutrition to the fore.

When Minty's father was knighted with a commemorative dinner in his honour filling the Strathcona Club Hall, I got up and gave a little bit of doggerel which people wanted me to repeat or to write down, but I thought it was so bad that I never had it on paper. However, just for the family, perhaps it is one of the things which might be of mild interest and so here it is:

"The farm and the Institute
Members who contribute
Work to bring nutritive knowledge to light
And the rest of Strathcona's Club
Are the donors here to commemorate
Pride in their knight;
Happy and glorious
Long to direct over us,
Sing we our wish
And feel we much more.
May never senility,
Let ever longevity
Honour the lives of the family Orr".

CAMBRIDGE/GOWLAND HOPKINS/ WALTER ELLIOT/BOYD ORR/ROWETT

At Cambridge when I had taken my Tripos degree, I applied to be on the biochemical course for another year. The staff were not very keen to have me because I had not done very well in the examinations and so they brought in "Hoppy" to their deliberations - Sir Frederick Gowland Hopkins, the man who demonstrated the vital need of animals for "accessory food factors" and one might almost say the father of vitamins and minerals. Hoppy asked me to see him and we had a talk together and of course he asked me what I was intending to do afterwards and I said I was going to go to a place called the Rowett Institute with the Director, Dr. Orr. Hoppy had not done too well in his examinations, like many famous people. He had just been up to the Rowett at the request of A.J. Balfour to find out if Dr. Orr was a genius or a charlatan. When he heard that Dr. Orr wanted me he had no hesitation in saying yes, I should have a place on the course. Hoppy was a delightful little man. Oddly enough, he had a sort of air force moustache, large, sticking out on either side, thick and twirled. When he was emphasising something, he used to rise up on his toes in a very characteristic fashion. He was a very important link in my career and I am eternally grateful.

My brother-in-law, Walter Elliot, was a man of great ability in the cut and thrust of the House of Commons. He had a highly developed memory like so many Scots who were brought up by their parents to learn passages of the Bible from an early age. I believe that it caused them to develop subconsciously some system of memory. He was very well read and as a doctor, a scientist and a politician he was a very useful man. When he became Minister of Agriculture in 1932 he took the previous Minister's ideas (the Socialist, Addison) and carried them through as the Agricultural Marketing Acts. He also held the office of Secretary of State for Scotland and when war broke out he was made Minister of Health. One of the major actions he was required to accomplish was the evacuation of the high density towns and cities.

There is in fact a good book by Colin Coote called "A Companion of Honour" - a biography of Walter. He was a polymath, i.e. he had a knowledge of many faculties of life. If a specialist came to talk to him on their subjects, he would be able not only to understand them but to have a meaningful conversation on their technical terms. He was very practically experienced in a few subjects - in World War I he'd had plenty of experience of medicine and surgery. He liked the good life to go with the good thinking. One never came away from a discussion with Walter without having learned something very worthwhile. He never, never rammed anything down one's throat. He enjoyed discovering other people's points of view on the subject and not infrequently he would introduce some information which had supported the view opposed to his own. Thus he learned to see all sides of any problem and this was his downfall politically. He was an excellent speaker in opposition. The way was straight, the other party was wrong and these are the reasons why. Period. He could marshal the reasons out of the depths of his brain on the spot in the House of Commons like nobody else could in his day. When it came to being a member of the party in power, things were different. He was one of a very interesting and active group in the Conservative party who had come back from World War I and were anxious to play their part in the peace of their country. Such were Harold MacMillan, "Shakes" Morrison and others. They were most of them deemed to be in the running for premiership. Anthony Eden was another one. Anyway, when problems cropped up on which decisions had to be made, some of the minority resigned on the basis of conscience. Walter didn't resign - in times of dissension he had great difficulties because he always saw both sides of the question. All this was happening under the eye of Winston Churchill and of course Winston, who was a rather hyper and intelligent man, saw this as a weakness in Walter and so long as he was in power, he never gave Walter the chances that he should have had.

He was a great gawky, clumsy creature and very short-sighted. At Harwood, his farm and estate, he used to have shooting parties - grouse over the hills, black game and a few pheasants in the winter and so on. He used to go out full of enthusiasm and would blaze away with his gun and never, never hit anything!

Walter was the most positive influence in my career. When he married my sister K in 1934 Boyd Orr and his wife were at the wedding. In his highly compelling manner, Walter said to Boyd Orr, "John you must take David into the Rowett". Reluctantly Boyd Orr acquiesced, or so it seemed to me. He told me to come up to the Rowett in the following summer. I arrived on the appointed day and found no-one at Wardenhill. I waited and waited until at last came a top-hatted man and a beautifully dressed lady back to their home. It had been John Crichton's wedding day. Obviously I had been totally forgotten, but he thought he had better have a talk with me. He asked me some roundabout questions and he couldn't really understand why I was there! He asked me "and why did you take up science at school"? "I'm not absolutely sure", I said, "but I think the main reason was that I knew I was lazy and that if I read history, which all my friends aimed to do because it was the easiest and didn't take up as much time as other subjects, I would be going down a lazy track and the future would not be good". We were both sitting in his study with our feet up on the mantelpiece. He brought his feet down with a clump and looked me straight in the eye. And from that moment on he thought that really there must be something in the man. So he said go away and come again on ...... (a date later in the year) which I did.

The first summer at the Rowett the International Physiological Congress was to be held in the USSR. Popeye couldn't go and nobody seemed to be free enough to go and everyone backed out, so it came down to my representing the Institute. Nothing loath, I did. I and a lot of the delegates to the conference, as well as I suppose the normal trade in passengers, embarked on a Russian boat in the Port of London with the destination of Leningrad. On the way I made friends with a young couple. He was working on vitamin B complex at Oxford. They had previously been in India. They are now in Edinburgh, Reg Passmore and his wife who affected large-brimmed hats. We arrived about the beginning of August or earlier at Kronstadt, the naval promontory and base which is about two miles out from Leningrad. We moved up channel from there and as the sun rose we could see Leningrad in all its glory - it was glorious because it was the first year of their cultural programme. All the spires had been re-gilded, everything that could be done in the time was done by then and when we arrived there was actually a red carpet and a band playing to greet us. It was the last year of Pavlov's life. He had been given charge of organising the conference which he did extremely well. In the main auditorium in Moscow he had simultaneous translation. When they got it in the United Nations and I was going through they said, have you heard this, it is wonderful - we have got this system and everything is translated at the same moment. Oh, I said, you mean simultaneous translation - I had that in Russia in 1933! Deflation of the UN staff present!

In August both in Leningrad and in Moscow it was terribly hot, but I think the conference as a whole was a success. It was the first international affair that the Soviets hosted.

BOYD ORR AND WORKING
AT THE ROWETT.

I am not going to attempt to cover the character of my father in law. His achievements are well known anyway and I was too close to him to be able to make an objective study that would be of value to people in the future. However, above all, he was a man who could wrench the fundamental truths out of a situation or the answer to any complicated problem. Whilst others were getting caught up in a cat's cradle of differences of opinion, he would break off to have fun with his family, play games, sing songs: he had a love of Scottish country dances but he once told me that he thought that apart from relaxation of that sort, it was a sin not to be thinking.

When I joined the Rowett and had got through the first phases of biochemistry, the rat studies, the human diet and physiology and so on, we used to work together, starting in the morning immediately after breakfast. I lived at the Rowett Institute and went across to Wardenhill for him and we walked up to Forrit Brae alone together discussing our long-term plans and then finishing up with what was the work of the day. Then we would go into the Institute and start in. I used to suggest one or two things which I would think were bright ideas of my own - about many of which he would say "Yes, I've thought of that". It was rather dampening and I wondered whether perhaps sometimes he hadn't! I think he saw this because one time, when I was suggesting something, he said yes, he had thought of that two years ago and he had taken this and that action and nothing had worked.

Whistling in the Institute was forbidden - he hated it. He would occasionally play the old-fashioned squeezebox (accordion) - he had a wonderful sense of rhythm. His parents had never allowed him to go to a dance. By the time he was free enough to do that on his own, he was tremendously taken with Scottish country dancing. This paid off for his daughter once. Judy (Dr. Elizabeth Orr) Barton ran out of cash in Dundee. She went to the Clydesdale bank and asked for some cash over the counter but the teller wouldn't let her have any as she seemed to have no means of identification. So, in anger, she said to the teller "My father is a director of yours". He told her to wait and buzzed off back to get the bank manager. It happened that ten days earlier or so there had been an annual "do" at the head office of the bank in Glasgow to which all the managers were invited - the bank manager came up to the window and said to Judy "What is your father's favourite dance?" She immediately answered "Petronella". He turned round to the teller and said give her all she wants!

The Director felt that a lot of the young staff were too conventional in their views and about life in general. He would be glad if I managed to move them a bit out of their custom thought processes. So at the Strathcona Club we'd talk after a meal or other odd moments and when somebody would make a statement saying "Obviously ...." and it did look obvious, I would challenge it. So people got to the point where they had to think twice before they would say something that they thought was obvious to me. Some of them used to say that I would make them think that white was black and black was white!

Boyd Orr became a member of parliament for the Universities of Scotland which was a wonderful seat for an Independent. He enjoyed his short time as a Member of the House of Commons. He was interested in and entered into the spirit of the tradition and the traditional behaviour suitable to the process of governing. I think it was a major wrench when he had to give it up to become Director General of FAO. He was pleased to be Lord Rector of Glasgow University and then to have had the honour of the Chancellorship bestowed on him when he was still Lord Rector. He took his duties as Chancellor very seriously and sensibly, I think. Once, when there were visiting foreigners to be honoured, he prepared a sentence for a Spanish poet who was to be capped; he trotted out his sentence in Spanish with the intention of carrying on to the capping of the next person right away, but the Spaniard wasn't going to miss his opportunity and started speaking to the Chancellor in voluble Spanish, not one word of which could Boyd Orr understand! Whoever was being capped, of whatever standing or age, he used to dunk them hard with his cap, making sure there was no mistake about it! (I wonder if we have his Lord Rector's speech, or any of the speeches as Chancellor? Don't think so.)

Once, coming out of the House of Commons with another MP who was rather stuffed-shirtish and talking to Boyd Orr in a very conservative, high fallutin' manner, they came across a policeman and Boyd Orr said to his colleague: "Oh, this is a relation of yours - I want you to meet him". The policeman was a Boyd and was related to Popeye in a very distant fashion and also claimed a relationship with the other man - and he didn't like it at all. It gave my father-in-law a good chuckle.

Another time, coming out of the House of Lords, he met up with the Provost of West Kilbride where he was born. The Provost had been well-lunched and Boyd Orr had been one of the two sponsors of the Head of ICI, Alec Fleck who had been elevated to the peerage; this was the day that he was introduced to the House and Popeye was one of the supporters - there had to be two, one on either side. When they were coming out (Minty's mother was there too) they got talking together as they stood on the steps waiting for a taxi; the Provost said that he had recently got a portrait of Alec Fleck and there was one of Popeye as well and the people in the Provost's Office in West Kilbride had asked him what should be done with them. He said he didn't know, but he thought he should hang "yon twa buggers at the end of the hall"!

He had a rich Scottish accent of the South West of Scotland and he spoke out very well. It was not only the words with which he managed to put over his message - it was the gestures too. People genuinely said "What a wonderful speech that was - I didn't understand a word he said but I am sure he is right"! He was slightly fey. When I had become a prisoner of war and nobody at home knew what had happened, within the first few days he got up from the lunch table and went through the door to listen to the radio on which Lord Haw Haw was mentioning the names of prisoners of war - after a brief time he came back and sat down and continued with his lunch and said "David's all right - he's a prisoner of war". How did he know to go and listen then?

I think he rather enjoyed his time in the Army during the war, first designing a reasonably hygienic camp for some large units in Kent and then going out on active service where he won the DSO and MC, a rare combination. He wouldn't wear his MC because he said that his batman had been with him all the time on this particular episode and he hadn't received any honour whatsoever for it. The batman was a Sherwood Forrester, a little chap who had been in a horse racing stables and was a jockey. When it came to procuring a horse, he got his batman to go along and choose a horse for him which he said was to be easily handled, but not too slow. He got him a beautiful horse which was known as Medical Molly until it was shot from under him. At one time behind the front lines in a tent, he found some strange, beautiful white gloves and various forms of equipment in the tent which he thought very odd and surely couldn't be his. Anyway he quizzed the batman and found out that he had gone round all his fellow officers' tents and picked up what looked best of all from them and put them in Boyd Orr's tent for him! The lad was made to pick them all up and return them to where he had found them and apologise.

I remember him telling me how he was in difficulties with some chap who was up to be court martialed for lack of moral fibre or something, so he went to see this chap and he wouldn't speak. He was obviously in shock and that would have been the end of him, but Boyd Orr made a joke which got through to him and he started to laugh and once he started to laugh out came the whole story. He hadn't actually shown any lack of moral fibre, so his life was spared.

His simple solution to trench feet was to return all the boots of his unit to be replaced by the same kind of boots one size larger. There was a general examination of trench feet - I don't know how often, just when it could be fitted in after coming out of the front lines, perhaps - anyway, his unit was called forward and he said there wasn't anybody. They said nonsense, that could not be, so they did a spot check and they couldn't find any trench feet!

I don't think he enjoyed the Navy so much on active service. He was on HMS Furious which, incidentally, was a converted cruiser aircraft carrier that went up with us - I was in HMS Victorious - for the Kirkness raid, but in World War I it was almost, if not actually, the first aircraft carrier in action. There wasn't any arrester mechanism on the flight deck and no arrester hook and so on, and a lot of unnecessary life was being lost and airplanes falling off the flight deck when landing, either one side or the other, or over the bows. I think I am right in saying that he wrote up and insisted on there being chains being stretched across the deck and some kind of hook for an arrester hook to be able to be lowered when landing on the flight deck in the hopes of it getting caught in the chain and the chain pulling the airplane up.

His eyesight was incredibly good - he could read a timetable or telephone book without any glasses until he was in his late eighties. When I was young he used to have a pair of pince-nez in his waistcoat pocket and you would say "Aren't the Grampian Hills lovely here" and he would pull them out and put them on his nose and say yes, wonderful - then he would fold them up again and put them back in his pocket again. He loved the beauty of the countryside. He loved the West Coast and the hills round West Kilbride. When I went to the Rowett there were some winters cold enough for the lochs to freeze over. Sometimes they would freeze over enough for skating and then there would be a Bonspiel. In the morning he would come round and look at what you were doing at your lab bench and then say "Well it can be left now for a bit can't it". You would say, no, not yet - "Oh yes it can", he would say and then he would gather enough of us to pile into a couple of cars and we would shoot off to Dinnet or wherever there was a Bonspiel going and we would skate. He used to love that - so did we all.

At Wardenhill, in addition to his family, he had his mother there and two sisters would come up fairly regularly from Saltcoats. Whenever he had property he put it in the name of one or other or both of the sisters. The paternal grandmother was a Clark and a lot of them had Clark as one of their names. There is a story there really: One of the Clark family was considered not bright enough to farm so he went off to Paisley and found work in the newly forming cotton industry. Clark managed the finances and the business J. & J. Clark; they merged with J. & P. Coats and grew into a big, transnational company. So the boy who wasn't clever enough to farm made an enormous cotton industry for Scotland.

The rival in cotton in those days was Germany which was in the forefront of developing modern techniques. It came down to a war between the two and J & P Coats lowered their prices in response to the Germans who had been undercutting them, who then lowered their prices again - I don't know how long this went on - 3 or 4 times - until the Germans couldn't take it any longer and they dropped out. Well,

Clark had arranged with the banks in Scotland that they could buy any quantity of cotton below a certain price, so whilst this was going on, surreptitiously cotton was being bought by agents for J. & P. Coats and the Germans went out of business. J. & P. Coats had made a corner in cotton thanks to Clark.

THE CARNEGIE SURVEY[6]

The Start

Lord Elgin, Head of Carnegie U.K. Trust, came to Sir John to ask advice about investing some extra money coming into the Trust Funds. Sir John suggested two alternatives:

a) further to develop a satellite township with people partly country, partly town. Object would be to take up vacancies in industry when there was demand and in farming at peak manpower times or b) to find out in more detail the nutritional health of the people of the U.K. then Food Consumption Survey (FCS) and Nutritional status studies and feeding experiments.

The Trust liked the latter idea and offered to fund such a project. Thus the Carnegie Survey.

The Help

Dr. H.E. Magee (Hughie), a medic who had been in the Rowett and was then in the Ministry of Health, played part guardian, part precursor. He recommended a Miss Dodds for leader of FCS teams. He paved the way at the civil service level for the entry of teams into districts to carry out the surveys. On the side of the Nutrition Survey we were lucky to have two excellent young medicos. The first was provided for us by Osborne Mavor (the author, James Bridie, who was a medical doctor at the Western Infirmary, Glasgow). There was a young doctor, Angus Thomson, who after the survey worked under Sir Dougald Baird, the celebrated gynaecologist

---

[6] This section was prompted by Bob Wenlock's visit, see p.16

who was an Aberdeen University professor. Angus later became a Professor at Newcastle University in the Faculty of Social Medicine. The second was Dr. John Pemberton. The how, why and wherefore of his joining us I don't remember. However, he and his wife fitted in very well because his wife acted as the Recorder for both the doctors' examinations of nutritional status.

Selecting Districts To Be Surveyed

These, quite frankly, were no more representative than broadly geographical and part rural, part town. They were, within that broad framework, the places where we were likely to get enough support to be able to carry out the work satisfactorily.

Attempts at Random Sampling

Our attempts, I think, were better than nothing. However, for your present purposes, I don't see that it matters much.

Rather than producing a statistical picture of the average UK man, or rather family, we hit upon one or two eccentricities in different places. These are probably recorded in the write up of each area, but at the moment I can think of two really outstanding ones which might be of interest to follow up if possible.

The first is that at Wisbech in East Anglia it was the custom among some mothers to breast feed for much longer periods than usual. In one instance I think there was found a boy who was still being breast fed at the age of seven years. I believe the women hoped it would prevent them from starting another pregnancy. Another was that at? (cannot remember at the moment) in the Midlands the children were given weak red wine to drink. It would be terribly lucky to be able to pick up any individuals who were representative of these idiosyncrasies, but the fact may make it possible to create new studies.

Criteria for Nutritional Status Assessment

Here we really were up against it. Since none of the criteria had a proven relationship to nutritional status, with the possible exception of heights and weights, we were really testing the criteria more than using the criteria as a standard for nutritional status. I felt it possible that we might be able to analyse the results in the sense of finding out something that had a positive correlation with nutritional status. From then on I was dogged by this difficulty. It stretched on into the nutritional status surveys that we managed to carry out in Zambia in 1969/70. All the criteria data or some of it, may be of use in analysis now. I can't tell that, but what would I not have given for your body mass index assessment in order to build up a simple, inexpensive, reliable and quick procedure for AFFA (Adequate Food For All).

As you know we were just finishing the field work when World War II was declared. I confess I never saw it myself, but Boyd Orr must have had access to see what was being prepared as a contingency plan for rationing in Great Britain. He was horrified. I was missing out on this because I was already being called up for training in the Fleet Arm. However we concentrated on getting out the results of the FCS side of the Carnegie Survey so that we could show what needed to be equitably distributed for the health of the people in terms of nutritional requirements. This was in relation to what food consumption surveys showed in terms of deficiencies. From this we could build up a specific food supplementary plan according to nutritional needs. With the data that we got from the Carnegie Survey we produced a tiny little booklet for the politicians entitled "Feeding the people in wartime" by Orr and Lubbock and I remember correcting the galley proofs in Portsmouth Barracks morning and evening in my hammock.

Work on the survey virtually closed down then. The Director, Boyd Orr was busy, so to speak, setting up Lord Walton as Minister of Food. All went very well from then on much, I suspect, to the chagrin of the Civil Servants who had lost their contingency plans for rationing. I was off to join No. 828 Squadron of the Fleet Air Arm.

Whatever in later research the Carnegie Survey might turn up of value, it had certainly paved the way for creating a logical basis for wartime rationing.

Two little anecdotes: first, children got milk, cod liver oil and orange juice. This originated in my mind from a lecture by Gowland Hopkins to us as undergraduates or graduates in biochemistry. He wrote up on the board what infants and children should have - this of course was about 1932 - in terms of one or two basic foodstuffs and he wrote up this list of very few foods: milk quantities, cod liver oil and orange juice. For brevity he wrote up "CLO" for cod liver oil and for the first five minutes looking at the list I could not think what CLO was! Anyway, those were some of the items I believe that were supplied to children during the war. I don't know much about it, of course, because I was a prisoner of war in Germany.

The other anecdote was one I heard some years after the war from a master of Gordonstoun School. It was when the war made everyone tighten their belts, institutions as well as individuals, and the Governing Body suggested to Dr. Kurt Hahn, the founder of Gordonstoun School, that money be saved by reduction in the quality of the food supply; in particular they seemed to think that the number of oranges going in to supply the school seemed rather excessive. Well, apparently, when this was brought to Dr. Hahn's attention he replied "Every boy (as it was then) shall receive, say, three oranges a week. David Lubbock says so!" And that was the end of that - those boys got their vitamin C!

After getting back from the war and being introduced by my wife to my daughter aged three and a half years, I started back to look into where I stood with the Carnegie Survey at the Institute. I was planning to write a report.

Obviously I have got to get my thinking cap on to get the chronology right here. Anyway I was back home in May 1945. The Quebec Conference took place in December 1945. My father-in-law asked me to go over to the States to help him set up the Food and Agricultural Organisation as he had been elected Director General thereof. Seeing that Part I of the Carnegie Survey, the food consumption surveys, had already provided valuable data for rationing for the people during the war, in trying to weigh up what I should do next, it seemed to me that I should go over to the States and help my father-in-law. Of course it was also a more invitingly exciting alternative! Thus I left the Carnegie Survey without a report. Much of the work that had to be done on a nutritional status survey was in the form of statistical correlations. I am not a statistician and I could not have done all that much myself. I could only have written the report, giving the story of the Survey and fitting its importance into the development of nutrition application to health.

While I was in Washington DC helping start up FAO the Rowett Institute prepared the report on the Carnegie Survey for the Carnegie Trust and also, of course, for general publication. I can't think of anything more to tell you but there may be more if you start asking me questions. The whole objective now is quite different, namely the follow-up of individuals to see what diseases crop up in adult life to children malnourished before and after birth. These modern analyses of correlation in human beings, of course, run parallel to what I had been saying for many years about animals. In cattle, if the calf didn't get the colostrum or if it was malnourished at an early stage, it didn't matter how well you fed that animal afterwards, its digestive processes would have been damaged by the malnutrition and it would never make use of all the nutrients required for a healthy animal because of this handicap, i.e. the development of the digestive system is handicapped by the malnutrition.

I don't think there is anything more I can say without questions to prompt me, but I hope that maybe one or two points I have made will be of use to your people in their analyses.

FAO - WASHINGTON DC

After the war when Minty's father was elected unanimously Director General of FAO, he wrote to me and invited me to join him. I dropped everything, we packed our bags and as a family - Ann Pat, Minty and me - set sail in one of the Queens from Liverpool and away we went. When we arrived in Halifax, I think it was, we transferred by train to Washington. I had far too much luggage in little bits of string bags and goodness knows what and as we got nearer to the time for the train to leave, the Red Cap asked me if I had checked my luggage. I said yes, I had but I will check it again if you like. I've got 14 pieces - and I started to count. Then I realised we were talking at cross purposes! He meant had I checked in my luggage with the luggage freight part of the train. This was the first example of the common language having different meanings.

When we got to Washington DC we booked into the Wardman Park Hotel and I started to look for a house to rent. After two weeks they threw us out - at that time they were not keeping any foreigners beyond the accommodation time. So we went to another hotel and it was during the post-war period when we could not take any of our capital out of the UK. We were therefore stuck especially since, comparing the cost of renting against purchasing a house, it would have paid hand over fist if we bought a house. So I discussed this with my father-in-law and he looked to see how much money he could spare and how much he could drum up out of FAO as DG, scraping the barrel, so to speak, and we managed to buy 5549 Thirtieth Place. It was a one up, one down and basement "pillbox". It suited us until our sons started coming along and the place became too small.

Once, when we were throwing a party, Florence Ignatieff, a very good Canadian friend (wife of Vladimir Ignatieff, son of the late Governor of Kiev and a wonderful man) rang Minty and said this is the police - I understand you are going to have a party tonight and that quite a few people are coming - how many do you think there will be? Minty said she was inviting 70, but she wasn't expecting so many and was very worried by the call; when she was thoroughly worked up, Florence started roaring with laughter on the other end of the telephone because it was just a practical joke. We had asked in Washington DC, if we were asking anything between 50 and 100 people what proportion we could expect to turn up and we were told the most would be 70% - so we worked out the space and that is how we came to the figure of 70 for invitations. Came the evening, more and more cars came, lining up round the streets, and we ended up with 69 people; 70 to start with because the Minister of Agriculture for Canada had to leave to catch a train and only came for a very short time. We had to open the basement which had a roaring fire going on all the time for the hot water etc. Nobody seemed to care; they all stayed and the party went on and on until we were both wet rags. We had Ann Pat, who was four years old then, dashing round with potato chips and I heard a lot of laughter at the other end of the room. I eased my way through the crowd to see what was happening: she had offered the plate to someone who had taken a chip and then she had said - "no, you've had one already!" She was used to the rationing at home!

I was taken off to business lunches in downtown Washington in the smart hotels and practically forced to take beef in a thickness and size which seemed abominable - it wouldn't even fit on the plate, but hung over the edge. I very nearly vomited the first time, then I managed to avoid getting into that state again.

Having pinched, borrowed, and been gifted loans and what have you in order to buy the house, Geoffrey was born 30th June. Space was becoming a real difficulty and so we looked around and found a place in Friendship Heights, across the DC line on the north side. We sold the house, paid everything off and bought the new house with a mortgage and we made a profit on the first house. For the rest of the five years we were in Friendship Heights and when we left we sold that and likewise made a profit. So it was worth all the effort, certainly scraping the barrel paid off compared with paying rent which might well have increased monthly.

The building we started in for FAO was a big private house on a hill. We had a staff of about 10. There were a lot of people milling about that the preparatory Commission had brought along in its wake and these people thought it would be very nice to have a job in FAO. This made it very difficult for my father-in-law. He didn't want any of them - he wanted his own men. This caused the rift between F.L. McDougal and the Director General. These people milled about and nobody did anything. Minty's father said he would need a car and nothing happened and he was told there wasn't any money for a car, which was ridiculous. He went to the guard on the door, a black man, and said "What is your name?" He said "William". "Well, William", he said, "go down to the nearest second hand car lot and get me the best car that you can there. You can drive and I'll make you my driver". So off went William and got a Packard and this made my father-in-law mobile.

It so happened that we all loved William and his wife, who looked after us in every possible way. When Boyd Orr resigned William wanted to come over with his family to Scotland, but it wouldn't have worked.

When the Director General started up in Washington DC he got a group of five or six representatives from different countries as a Cabinet to keep him from straying too far from their peoples' ways: there was one each from China, S. Africa, France (Professor Andre Mayer, celebrated physiologist whose son is now the head of Tufts) and Egypt (Hefnawy Pasha who was a very staunch supporter - I liked him from the start and I liked him better still when he told me that he had read everything that my great uncle had ever written and was a great admirer of his).

From the time of introducing nutrition into international affairs, from the League of Nations onwards to the formation of FAO and its first three years, we aimed high. To have succeeded would really have been a miracle. The only thing was to wait until the world got itself into such a mess that leaders would have to look back at the Boyd Orr proposals and act.

Starting up FAO was not easy. In the first three years when he was Director General and the staff was small, he would go round and see what people were doing in their offices and what were the major problems that they were coming up against. He would sometimes come into my room and looking at the work, ask me "Can it wait?" - "Well, how long?" "Oh, half an hour or so". "Yes, Sir". "Then I want you to come along with me". We would walk out of the building across the street into a little coffee shop, stand in the queue for a cup of coffee and then sit down unmolested by the staff of FAO we would run over how things were going division by division.[7]

At the early stages there was very little cohesion. I would perhaps get my cue that, say, the forestry division was trying to pull a fast one in trying to build their little empire. Later that day or the next day I would go and see the director of the division and quietly let him know that I knew what he was up to and that he wouldn't be able to get away with it. No further trouble.

I remember one day in the coffee shop he said "Davey, lad, sometimes I think this job is impossible and then I think on what a thin, tenuous line Abraham Lincoln held on to and eventually won through". Years later I was told when the top level of administration of FAO in Rome got in a tangle it was suggested by more than one division director that the Director General and the Directors of the Divisions needed someone to talk to as the DG and directors had to me in the early days. We both had the same somewhat altruistic objective probably best summed up as a World Food Authority. We each had very different roles to play. Boyd Orr was, I think, very careful to avoid any suggestions of nepotism.

He only took half the salary that was due him as Director General and at the end of the first financial year he had saved enough to put aside quite a quantity of capital for the agency. Of course this was fairly easy when you couldn't get things going and your expenditure did not meet up with your budgeting. But he was very disappointed when not one single person congratulated him on running a specialised agency of the world at a saving rate.

---

[7]   Popeye and I went to work/talk in a café and realised we had been invited to lunch with the Russian ambassador, Ivan Mikhaylovich Mayskiy. (I had been invited to dinner with Vivian Smith's daughter to which the Russian ambassador had also been invited. Naturally the subject of USSR and food had come up and the ambassador had started quoting statistics, and I had said I was most interested, so Mayskiy said he would arrange for me to come to lunch). Too late, we had missed it. I had to write an apology. Mrs. Mayskiy wrote back to say that the behavior was so Russian that she would like me to come to tea.

Staff recruitment was extremely difficult - there were too many Americans and too many British who had been active at the Quebec conference and who, after the setting up of the preparatory commission by the Hot Springs Conference, were more than half promised a job in the Secretariat. Even if they were all worth it, you couldn't have them all because there was a quota according to the contributions of the countries. Also, immediately post-war, the best people of every country were needed and being employed by that country to re-establish their social and economic fabric. Consequently when you asked for Professor X or Mr. Y who was high up in the government circles of a member nation, the reply would be "you can have anyone else, but not him". It was very natural. The Boyd Orr proposals were being prepared. Meanwhile two good missions were carried out, first one in Greece and then one in Poland as well, of course, as working up the divisions. We were shortly landed with a dilemma. The more the delegates recognised that something was going to have to be done about population control, the more all the countries in the world that were Roman Catholic - including the main bulk of Latin America - told the DG privately that if he were to speak out more in that direction, they would drop membership. It was obvious then that birth control would have to come in eventually but the lesser of the two evils was to carry on without emphasising it and waiting until the climate was suitable for talking about birth control, which has taken more than 40 years. Meanwhile, in that time, the world population has increased enormously.

He was devoted to his wife and took her everywhere with him on his expeditions for the Empire Marketing Board round the world and at FAO when he went visiting different nations; whenever he could he took her with him. She was a tremendous stand-by because she was very, very sensitive and very clever - so clever that you would never know it. If Boyd Orr got tangled in a discussion or argument during the day and there were drinks in the evening, she would be able to go to the man who, one might say, had been causing the trouble or expressing a minority view, and who might be looking rather wretched; she would draw him in with the others and have them all laughing within five minutes - people who were apparently deadly opposed to one another. It was a miracle to watch. He knew her judgement of human beings was better than his and he took her advice on every conceivable subject, except nutrition and medicine. She disagreed with him instinctively over this, it seemed - anyway she never accepted his word, which rather tickled him.

Now perhaps we are in a better position to look at the major trends that were influencing thought about contemporary world society. First there was the euphoria that we were getting a United Nations organisation which would be able to dissolve the bones of contention. But then the empire building of the UN organisations capable of producing the paper work but incapable of managing and controlling the global problems resulted in hotbeds of international diplomacy and money for the boys who could get into it. At this point it must always be said that there was a small proportion of personnel in field work and in headquarters who were sweating their guts out to make a proper go of things. A year or so after Boyd Orr managed to get out from under, he would say "Davey, lad, I am glad we have got out from all of this". From then on we were not in the same boat.

BOYD ORR/LUBBOCK PARTNERSHIP

I don't think he ever showed me how to do anything. He knew he could ask me to tackle anything after *Food, Health & Income*. There - I asked for it. First we went round together to ask help from departments of Ministers such as the whereabouts of food consumption studies made within the previous 4 years. Boyd Orr explained what he was aiming to do and therefore why he needed specific help from them. They said they understood and we left. I then followed up with more specific details on his requests. They then would say to me that what he wanted to be done could not be done and therefore there wasn't any point and I should give up. I would indicate that we were going to go ahead and try anyway. That usually let them off the professional civil service hook after which they would say that they personally would help all they could. Gradually "can't be done" turned into "can do".

I think it was this aspect which made him ask me to join him at FAO. Anyway, he landed me with a wallop right away. He was determined FAO, the top world food body, should not turn a blind eye to gathering famines due to war and post-war disturbance of food production and supply. The British expected FAO to turn a blind eye. It was "not their job" [which was] only long-term and advisory functions. Then we came slap bang up to the philosophy crisis: make and keep FAO ineffective in solving world food problems or take the objective of feeding the world adequate diets no matter what it takes.

We needed the facts of the world food situation there and then. Who could give him the data? "Ask Mr. Lubbock to come in" (to a meeting mainly of US and UK civil servants). Boyd Orr: "Mr. Lubbock, will you be prepared to put together an assessment of the present world food situation?" I was not long back from having been 3 years, 9 months a POW in Germany. To me most things seemed impossible. "How accurate? How soon?" Answer: "Within 4 months" "I shall need a lot of outside help". USDA, Bureau of Agri. Econ. as it was then called, offered help. After a short talk with Howard Tolley he gave me his No.2 Oris Wells (later to become DDG). All right. We should at least be able to paint a more accurate picture than anyone else.

It was a terrifying responsibility for me. Boyd Orr knew one thing - that I wouldn't fudge the results. I put Oris Wells at a desk opposite and adjacent to mine. His rapid mode of speech was difficult enough for his own people. After we had been passing paper between each other for two weeks we both had to admit that neither of us knew what the other was saying. However, we got it done and on time with the help, or sometimes hindrance, of the State Departments' food data coming in from Embassies and Legations. Of course it wasn't accurate, but better than anyone else could do, so we did have fairly reliable data. It was a good enough basis from which to get agreement to set up IEFC - The International European Food Council.

Of course once Boyd Orr was out of the way, the IFEC was terminated instead of being built upon.

Boyd Orr told me (in the 1950s) that he loved me as if I were his own son. In the winter evenings we used to sit by the fireside, with our feet up on the mantelpiece, heart and brain almost at the same level. We didn't seem to need to use words much when striving to think things through. As a result the family used to joke that as we sat or lay there, one of us would grunt and the other would maybe grunt back!

Isabella Leitch also had an instinctive understanding of what we were trying to do and was often a lot more practical and logical in her reactions. We never needed to express in high fallutin' terms and words what was the ultimate objective. But we all three recognised what was the next step to be taken. And we all three played very different parts on the way to get there.

He would give me his lectures etc. before delivering them. If I found a problem, in other words if I didn't understand anything, he would just say "Cut it out." That's how the terseness came into his writing. If there is a problem in comprehension, it's not going to be quite right. I often thought he was being too soft, I being more to the left than he. He would often accept a suggestion and it would sometimes end up being the lead point of the presentation.

After he resigned from FAO Boyd Orr was working from the top downwards. He visited a number of countries at the request of the Prime Ministers or Presidents. He was responding to requests by leaders of nations for him to investigate and report directly to them to advise them on how to manage their national food situation. In Pakistan, I remember, he advised that they put the whole programme under the military, the reason being that there was no organisation in Pakistan which was incorruptible enough to run a programme.

After 1951 when I resigned I worked from the grassroots upwards. I was responding to requests by FAO to visit member countries as a consultant to help to improve the food situation for their peoples. In the Far East I went to Indonesia; in Latin America I went to Colombia and to Mexico and in Africa I went to Zambia where the proposals I put forward were accepted and I was asked to go out as a project manager for the proposals I had made. I became convinced of the need for an integrated approach if viable improvement in nutrition were to be effected. This cannot be achieved without co-ordinated United Nations action to help the country or group of countries concerned. I have tried to indicate how this can be done starting with food adequacy under a global commitment and to a programme objective which I have called AFFA, Adequate Food For All.

If we had not been coming to the end of our lives, we would have written a book. This would have gathered together the flood tide of new global, youthful thinking to give it a positive, creative side with an objective for world co-operation rather than the present negative side of restricting pollution etc. It is needed because no-one is giving a positive lead to public opinion and as the UN and its specialised organisations generally are ineffective, so the commercial and business transnational institutions and companies are moving in to take their pickings. As it was we could only manage "From the Old World to the New". The alternatives are world food trade and wars for profit, or a new world order based on providing an adequate diet for all, an objective for which all peoples can co-operate and bring the products of science for the benefit of humanity. The gloves are off, the fight is on.

APPENDIX I

WORLD COOPERATION DEVELOPMENT

Empire Marketing Board

About the end of the 1920s, I think I am right in saying, the Empire Marketing Board was set up with a considerable fund at its disposal. The Board consisted of men outstanding in their field. The objective was the development of an Empire economy which could expand throughout the Dominions and Colonies and raise the standard of living for all. It was as part of this that Boyd Orr was sent round the Empire and indeed to other countries to develop an Empire Science Network. Out of this grew the formation of Imperial Bureaux such as Imperial Bureau of Animal Nutrition. Boyd Orr proposed the idea in Whitehall where it was "damned with faint praise". This goaded him into announcing that he would start the Imperial Bureau of Animal Nutrition at the Rowett. The Rowett would produce a periodical - "Nutrition Abstracts and Reviews". They would ask for no government funds. The start was shaky as far as I know - it was before my time but they won through. Then came the conference in Canada - Ottawa I think - to discuss the potential of development of marketing in the Empire. However, the result as described by Boyd Orr was that they just sat down and discussed relative prices of pots and pans! Here was an opportunity thrown away, an opportunity to develop the well-being of this vast Empire and thence the possibility of extending it to the whole world. Boyd Orr tried again after the war. As Director General, he spoke to Atlee as Prime Minister and painted the picture of how Great Britain could take the lead in developing the new world order - that is what it amounted to. Atlee, incidentally, told him that he had never heard anything about FAO - he didn't know what it was. The Civil Servants had kept it away from him and there was so much else to do on the short-term crises due to the dislocation of war, no doubt.

About 1947 Boyd Orr went to Harry Truman who was president of the United States at that time. He, too, knew very little of FAO and the Boyd Orr proposals. I attended neither of these meetings, so am vague about them. But the facts are that these leaders knew nothing (and were kept from knowing anything by their own Civil Services) about the embryo efforts to produce a new world order based on the advances of science for the benefit of all. They were completely caught up by the fear of a third world war and how to limit arms and armaments. They did not realise that the people of Russia, after the ghastly losses that they had incurred, and the terrible deprivations, would not have gone to war under any circumstances no matter who was leading from the Kremlin. They would not have fought. Yet the American fighting services were pressing the President to go and fight the Russians before they got the bomb - and by fight, I mean use the bomb on Russia. The objectives of the Atlantic charter have failed. In the objective of preventing wars there have been wars in three figures since the end of World War II. Not only failure there, but failure to give power to the administration of the United Nations on the positive side to make available to all the people the benefits of science to improve the quality of life.

In the 1950s and '60s we began to realise that if Governments would not co-operate to make the United Nations and its Specialised Agencies work, then these UN bodies would become demoralised and corrupted.

Frank McDougall

F.L. McDougall, CMG, was on the Empire Marketing Board, presumably representing Australia. He was invited to a Rowett Founders' Day at which he walked around the labs seeing what people were doing. He came to look over my work and asked questions which showed he was interested in what I was doing. He said he was and I said that I would go and get the details of my work and go over it with him, which we did. We began to talk about malnutrition in the Empire and in the world as a whole. It was thus that Frank brought me into his circle. He radiated enthusiasm and wrote copious memoranda which he used to send to those in the circle. He did this to such an extent that people got fed up. However, the memoranda were really so good that people could not really neglect what he had to say. Eventually he managed to get Viscount Bruce of Melbourne and Earl Delaware from the Ministry of Agriculture, UK, to introduce nutrition into the Assembly of the League of Nations. The League debate was a success, lasting the three days, to the astonishment of the international civil servants and others and it was agreed to set up a Commission. Frank managed to get Lord Waldorf Astor to take the chair of the Commission and it was agreed with Boyd Orr that I should go out as the advisor to Lord Astor.

I think it must have been the high heidyins of the UK civil service who tried to stop Astor. While we were in London a Medical Officer of Health came along to talk to him and Waldorf asked me to sit in and this man held forth that there wasn't any malnutrition anywhere in the world - certainly wasn't any malnutrition in Britain and there was no longer rickets in Glasgow and so -forth. I just let him ramble on. Waldorf was not all that clever, but he knew where things stood and we had a good laugh after he left - and that's saying a lot, because Waldorf Astor hardly ever laughed!

United Nations: why has it failed and been so weak?

I am prepared to give the architects of the UN Organisation the benefit of the doubt that they meant for the Technical Assistance Board or a Preparatory Commission of the United Nations to be the co-ordinating body of the Specialised Agencies. Through this body it would have been possible to have created an integrated approach to the development of the Third World. Lord Bruce of Australia wanted to head it up. I don't know the details of why he did not get it but it looks like the same story of the nations of the world being too frightened to make the United Nations work. Because of that the Secretary General was always chosen as a compromise because the man whom the Soviets wanted, the Western world wouldn't have, and vice versa. Anyway it was given to a Mr. Owen who, I think, said in print that he did not feel he was capable of the post. He was a very good, honest man but he hadn't the qualifications for knocking the heads of the directors general of the specialised agencies together and making them work in an integrated fashion. As a result of that, each went off and built their own empires all over the world. I believe that if we can get past the governments and the establishments of the dictatorships that govern and lead the peoples of nations - past the politicians and the diplomats, I am optimistic that there are people in practically every country of the world, who, given the vision would work to make the United Nations machinery function - graft is one of our main hurdles.[8]

An illustration of the different attitude to and uses of "graft" was exemplified by the Chinese; Dr. Chen wanted FAO to pay for his travel all the way from his base in China. I knew that he had come to the States on another purpose as well and that his travel had been paid for from this other source, so I just arranged that he should be paid his due as far as FAO was concerned for his travel. He got extremely angry and discovered that I was the trouble so he thought that he would haul me over the coals and of course he thought he would then get the whole fare paid by FAO. He said he was going to go to the DG about this matter - that was the last I heard of the matter!

In a fortuitous way in Colombia when I was there the Dictator was a Generalissimo Rohas Pinea. I of course had to work through the Colombian government. I had a very good Colombian medical man as my opposite number, but I could not get anything going with the medical profession. I was getting balked - I could do a certain amount on the food production and distribution side, but I was balked on the medical health side. Mark you, I always tried to work with the WHO representative, but it always seemed that wherever I went, field workers were instructed to have nothing to do with FAO. When I used to barge in to them and say

---

8   Write up Health section of the League's M_____ and Ayckroyd Report [possibly E. Burnett and W.R. Aykroyd "Nutrition and Public Health" League of Nutrition's Quarterly Bulletin of the Health Organization, 1935] which is basic and 2) pursue the subject of birth control amongst the Roman Catholics in Latin America where I found that numbers of priests felt that it was more of a sin to bring children into the world in utter poverty as was happening there than the birth control itself. Of course they had no objection to abstinence and in that sense birth control is no sin. We should look out particularly for the M_____ & Ayckroyd Report, and also for Popeye's letter to me asking me to join him in Washington.

let's work together, they couldn't understand it... but that is by the way. My point is that, since I was getting nowhere with the medical profession, I decided to go and see the doyen of the medicos. He agreed to see me one evening in his private house. So I went along and he received me coldly and I had to put forward my side of the story in Spanish and gradually he began to see that what I was trying to do was for the benefit of the people not for Rohas Pinea. He stopped me and said in English, are you any relation to Sir John Lubbock, and I said, yes he was my great uncle and he said, "I've read everything that your great uncle ever wrote and I am a great admirer of him. Now what is it you want of the medical profession here?"

Since we are on to Colombia, I'd like to make another point. It is one of general significance, but this is an incident in particular that happened. I had to leave Colombia to get back for something in Britain or Rome - not sure what. In fact, I'm not sure it wasn't that Rohas Pinea was thrown out in a revolution. I was there for that, so I don't think it could have been that. Anyway, when I came back, I connected with my opposite number, a Doctor who belonged to a great coffee-trading family, and we went over what he had been able to do while I was away. I had told him that I had to break off but that I would be back four months later and that in that time I thought it would be a good idea to get this started, and to do that and so on - I piled it on. Anyway, when I came back, I asked him how things had gone and I was amazed how much he had managed to do in a country where mañana ruled and things didn't happen very quickly. So I said how could you possibly manage to do all this. He looked me straight in the eye and said "I knew you were coming back". I believe it to be of great importance that in helping people to help themselves you give them a start, and you leave them to do something which is fairly well within their capacity; if when you come back they have done well, you encourage them and you move them on to another stage and that is the way that in the end they can take full responsibility themselves.

Integrated programmes

It was Dr. Platt who when asked what single thing would help improve nutrition in the poorer countries, replied the building of roads. Integrated programmes are essential. The first two missions, in fact the only missions, as far as I can remember, of FAO in Europe both emphasised the need for integrating planning and programming. The first was in Greece, and the second in Poland. The fact that these missions were not to poorer countries in the Southern Hemisphere, for example, might seem odd. The reason is that action as a result of the findings and reports of the missions would involve money from the world bank - The International Bank for Reconstruction and Development. The bank's own fund was, and is, dependent on public investment in the bank for its sources of funds and in those early days - about 1946/47 the establishment of the bank was about as shaky as the establishment of FAO. Dr. Black, the Director General of the World Bank could only get public investment support for projects reasonably likely to be able to give a return at the then going rates of interest. When Boyd Orr pressed Black for co-operation in developing the needy countries, his answer was that at that time he could not do it. We would have to wait until the world had got confidence in the IBRD.

The Boyd Orr proposals for lending money to needy countries was far from being acceptable to the rest of the world [countries would not have to repay the loans until their economies were strong enough for them to do so]. Of course this is what has happened in the very worst way: money has been lent, reconstruction has not taken place sufficiently, the developing country has not been able to pay back - first the interest has had to be written off, and then the very loan itself.

Of course, later on when oil popped out of the ground and the people of the oil producing countries recognised that their wasting asset was being plundered, a more equitable value of oil was marked up. The oil rich countries became suddenly very wealthy and though the western world's economy had to take the strain of the much higher price, new markets for Western products opened up in the oil rich countries. If the price of other wasting assets in demand by the western world was raised, more could be achieved on similar lines. It could be done for ore, tin, manganese, copper, all the metals - phosphate rock and anything hewed out of the ground. I think it was Samuel Hoare who recognised this way back in the mid-1930s when he suggested that the world's basic resources should belong to everyone. This may not be accurate, but the point is he was seeing something through a glass darkly - he was never able to explain it properly, and people didn't understand or dared not say it. It is essential to build up assets in the needy countries. This would lead to expanded opportunities for these populations – improved health would lead to an increase in manpower, then production, then purchasing power.

For the next stage in global organisation and administration, we have to think about personnel and "worldsmen" able to take charge. Presumably in December [at the international conference] there will be at least some statesmen and out of some of those statesmen there might be a proportion of worldsman-minded people. The qualifications for worldsmen capable of taking charge may seem to be superhuman. But there are latent abilities which can be brought out and we have to think about education to produce suitable people. This is more important than struggling away with how we may best manage to teach the three Rs to the masses. The Russians have thought about it and the Chinese have thought about it, and they have both taken action. In USSR I think it broke down. In China, who knows? There is no doubt in my mind that China will become the top nation. She has a significant proportion of all the wasting assets in the world and she has a quarter of the population of the world. If she but sees it, she can become top nation without firing a shot.

1992 - THE CRUX I BELIEVE IN THE PRESENT CRITICAL PREDICAMENT IN WORLD FOOD MANAGEMENT.

This has to be tackled as a crusade. The Body Mass Index is a powerful tool and can be used to coax and cajole nations into serious action on world food management. There needs to be a vast UN University, with national universities making up a special faculty for global issues. The core of the university would be the business of integration: e.g. forestry with roads, water with malaria and so on. It is then easy to see how to get rolling: an integrated team from the UN University comes in and examines aspects on a global basis. There must be money, of course, but as a convenient measure, but not as an object of profit in itself. That should go for ever, otherwise things are impossible. Weigh against that the wonderful new world that we can make by applying our knowledge and distributing and building up the education and the health of the people concerned, as well of course as putting top priority on birth control.

I think that compulsory service overseas for the young people would be a very good thing to start with and it might well be politically acceptable. I think the most important early action must be within the United Nations, creating a training ground for integration. This would take a lot of time to perfect but once objectives and targets are agreed, there would be something to work for. We now need to startle people into global thinking. Of course budget figures must look absolutely gigantic, but then politicians are not used to looking at things globally. Some of the transnational companies are not frightened of thinking this way, and they may be a bit tricky.

Don't ever be put off by people saying "it can never be done". The things that I put most to my credit and my satisfaction are things which I was told could not be done. You face up to the situation; you work for an objective; the closed gates start to open a little and gradually more and more progress results.

Education: It is a mistake to confuse educating with training. To my mind, educating is enabling a person to use as much of his inherited mind as possible. Training is a method of making individuals conform to a pattern and moulding them into a form of custom thought.

An idea relating to the conference in December in Rome: write to the President/Chairman of the meeting putting forward a plea for radical action along these lines:-

"Having been directly concerned with the introduction of food and nutrition into international affairs at the League of Nations before World War II in the 1930s may I, Mr. Chairman, make a plea that your conference face the critical world food situation currently arising and determine to take radical action on a global basis to create a World Food Authority with powers similar to those outlined by Lord Boyd Orr in 1946 to provide adequate food for all [AFFA]? Although unfortunately I was not directly concerned with the setting up of the Food and Agriculture Organisation, I worked in the Headquarters of FAO and in the field as a consultant and project manager. From my deathbed, I charge you, the knowledgeable ones, who can engender the will among the people if you care to".

If we got something going like this, improved of course, we could perhaps make an impact at the beginning of the meeting itself. I am thinking in much too vague terms but along the lines of this being a letter to be given to the British representative to ask the Chairman to read out. It should be addressed to the Chairman but brought up through the British delegation, if they would agree, so that it would not be lost. Maybe it should be an open letter where we could have at the same time copies of it distributed throughout the intelligent press - or the tabloids as well for that matter.

Of course, the man to put it across vocally in song is Andrew Lloyd Webber. He obviously has a picture of the future in his mind's eye and ear. If he were taken on with the AFFA idea he could write popular lyrics and music. I am thinking in the first instance of songs based on "Think globally, sing globally, act globally" etc., and then something around AFFA. Maybe I am too optimistic, but we have a long way to go and a short time to do it, so we have to try everything.

We start in 1945, '46, '47 when hunting for support for the Boyd Orr proposals for a World Food Authority. In a nutshell the diplomats and the civil servants of the major national powers pooh-poohed the idea through fear of loss of national sovereignty and anyway they said the whole idea was pie in the sky - altogether outside their accustomed thinking. I have no evidence of this because I wasn't in any of the discussions, but Boyd Orr told me later business people at the top quickly grasped the whole idea. At the same time, of course, they would recognise the potential for the profits for their individual companies if they could get in on the act. From then on we realised that if the nations of the world would not co-operate to create a World Food Authority, there remained rich pickings for them.

Food trade companies sail very close to the wind, they are very careful about not leaving evidence of malpractice. I am afraid that I do not have anything hard and fast. I do remember being told in 1929 or early 1930s that when there was a controversy about hygiene of milk that one or more commercial dairy companies tried, and in some cases I believe succeeded, in paying "scientists" to write articles in favour of pasteurisation on purely scientific grounds. Companies had so much profit to gain by the increased tanker life of pasteurised rather than fresh milk. In those days among the poor the diet was so bad that we felt milk of almost any state of hygiene and twice the quantity currently being consumed would be beneficial to health.

In 1945 when we were living in Washington DC skimmed milk was being sold at a high price as a health product and cream was very expensive. On the whole however, I think the American government was more advanced than those of other countries in legislating to avoid the conning of the public by the food industry. This was being assiduously tackled by Dr. Hazel K. Steebling in her unit of the US Department of Agriculture. They started mandatory food labelling, whereby the nutritional content of the food is shown.

In the immediate circumstances of 1992 it looks as if it will be impossible to whip up enough popular drive for so bold an aim as AFFA. An alternative to be examined is on the basis of the food trades - if you cannot beat them, join them. Or rather it means get big Agri-business companies to join together to sink their competitive differences to some extent and for them to agree to co-operate in a programme with a great objective to achieve adequate food for all. There would be much more profit in such a programme than in what I believe they are trying to do now, namely suborn the Specialised Agencies for each trade to get the UN machinery to work for their particular competitive advantage.

Political leaders are not interested unless they have to be. National civil servants are dead against it because of their loyalty to the national sovereignty; however they also see that if an international civil service organisation were to become effective, they would become very small beer by comparison in their own countries. The answer is the youth and the transnational companies. These are the two groups on which we must work. The former to enlist their enthusiasm and support for the latter to work out ways and means by which our objective can be reached with the help of the food trades and other trades. It being shown to be in the long run more worthwhile than their present policies.

We need to be able to affect public opinion. There is a greater number of enthusiasts interested in saving endangered species. Their thoughts need to be guided toward the idea that in reality human beings are an endangered species. There are too many on the planet, straining resources; a combination of effective birth control policies and improved access to food and nutrition will slow the trend. The first step is the establishment of a World Food Authority.

We have an example of the problem with the re-election or not of Mr. Delors in the European Community. Incidentally, when the Treaty of Rome for the European Community was coming into being, Aidan Crawley said to me that I must be very pleased to see this coming about. To his surprise, I told him that I was not pleased. The prime objective was to create a Unit or united group of countries with power more akin to that of USSR and USA, thus the old game of balance of power politics could be continued. It was a retrograde step to a system which, as history shows, can inevitably lead to war (when the balance of power comes out of balance). Thus the European Community idea was a bite at the cherry of global administration, retrograde and dangerous. That was my opinion.

Nevertheless, the thinking, the formation and the growth of the Community have provided a lot of lessons about administration of discrete countries with different environmental and different social structures - that has been made abundantly clear in trying to get a CAP [Common Agricultural Policy]. FAO has tried to encourage the formation of socio-economic groups in regions such as the Far East, Africa and Latin America and so forth. In forestry and fisheries they tried to set up councils such as Councils of the Seas amongst other things, to prevent plundering, with limited success.

This reluctance amongst all people is I think made use of by national civil servants. Civil servants act within their own purview, namely to improve their own nation's welfare - this makes it all the harder. I see no future in tackling this difficulty head on. The right way of getting there is to have enough enthusiasm and will to accomplish an objective. And the World Food Authority is the right one to press for. That should take top priority now. What kind of relationship between national civil service and international civil service would be needed? That will just be solved by what turns out to be necessary in the pursuance of the World Food Authority objective.

The human race will look pretty silly in terms of the cosmos if, with all the advantages it has on planet Earth and with the scientific knowledge it has so far managed to acquire, sufficient to introduce a new world order of plenty for all, we do not apply the necessary administration and controls. We degenerate and become extinct, like all the millions of other species that have become extinct before us.

For me, number one is to think of anything in my experience of the past that will be helpful to Philip [James]. Then I think I should prepare a list of essentials for the improvement of nutrition in countries or groups of countries. Here the United Nations members must be in agreement with the principle of helping the countries most in need nutritionally. The selection today with the tools we have is easy - body mass index and food balance sheets. Then it must be realised that, whatever the cost of the project, the cost of not carrying it out is greater. Then an integrated programme has to be worked out. For example, locusts breed in one country then eat the crops belonging to another. Both countries must cooperate to solve the problem. Payment for the help must not be the exporting of the capital value of the country's minerals, ores. If it is in loans at a certain rate of interest it has to be paid back only when the country has improved its productivity to a point where it can do so without ruining it own economy. Possibly export of labour might be one way of helping to pay. There has to be training of the people of the country from the top government level down. At the same time there has to be training from the grassroots level up. Here is where "compulsory volunteer service overseas" comes in. Happiness can be brought by individuals helping other people. Also by going into the villages and discussing things with village headmen and living lives the same as the villagers, introducing improvements of one sort or another which the people can copy. Success at the grassroots in one village can stretch to imitation up to a radius of 50 miles.

APPENDIX II

NOTES & THE ROYAL

RECORDS OF SOCIETY

The Forgotten Man: Sir John Lubbock, F.R.S.

R. J. Pumphrey

Notes Rec. R. Soc. Lond. 1958 **13,** doi: 10.1098/
rsnr.1958.0005, published June 1, **1958**

THE FORGOTTEN MAN—SIR JOHN LUBBOCK, F.R.S.
By R.J. PUMPHREY F.R.S.

WHEN Sir John Lubbock, 1ˢᵗ Lord Avebury, died in 1913 (before the outbreak of the 1914-18 war) he was deeply mourned by thousands who knew him and revered by millions who only knew of him. By the end of that war his reputation was in complete eclipse and it is only now and very partially beginning to emerge from an unmerited obscurity.

In a recent number of *New Biology* I found the following passage: 'It is remarkable that up to 1914 there was no definite proof that bees could see colours. Everyone from Sprengel onwards had assumed it, but there were only a few experiments such as those of Lubbock (1875-6). These, though suggesting that bees possessed colour-vision, did not eliminate the possibility that they discriminated between different colours by their brightness alone. Indeed, the first full-scale experiments came from Hess (1913) who claimed that this was the case: that honey bees could not see true colours but only various shades of grey. For a time there was doubt, but in 1914 von Frisch began his classic work.

This is one example of how Lubbock's work is forgotten or, if remembered, described in such a way as to diminish its importance. It is simply not true that von Frisch proved what Lubbock had failed to prove forty years earlier. Von Frisch does not mention Lubbock in his bibliography and it may well be that he was only impelled to begin his colour-vision work by a distrust of the work of Hess who started out with a bee in his bonnet and was wrong about most things. Nevertheless, von Frisch's technique resembled Lubbock's very closely and his results are open to the same sort of criticism. The final answer was given so far as bees are concerned, not by von Frisch in 1914, but by Kuhn in 1927 using pure spectral colours (a method invented by Lubbock though applied by him only to *Daphnia* and to ants). It is worth noting that Lubbock's experiments on bees were supported by extremely pertinent observations on the colour-sensitivity of wasps and ants, water-fleas and dogs. Lubbock answered contemporary criticism temperately and convincingly. He can hardly be blamed for not replying to the effusions of Hess which in any case were not published till he was dying. Nothing subsequent should be allowed to obscure the fact that Lubbock was the first by forty years to do experiments in this field, and that he got answers which as far as they went, were absolutely right.

Yet, when I took a course in zoology at Cambridge in the twenties, although my pastors and masters spoke highly of the virtues of the experimental method (held by some of them to be a Cambridge invention), I never heard Lubbock mentioned. It is true that I never heard von Frisch mentioned either, and the extraordinary post-war development of comparative physiology in Germany passed almost unnoticed. Until I began to read for myself, I did not realize how much Lubbock had done, not only in his experiments and in pointing the way to further work, but in creating the climate of opinion in which experimental work in biology was possible. The obscurity into which Lubbock's work lapsed after the 1914-18 war did not, however, cover only his contribution to zoology. He had been eminent, indeed pre-eminent, in many fields and, in all, his work seemed to be forgotten. I am not competent for the reappraisal which is overdue, but it seems worth while to glance, however superficially, at his extraordinary career and to try to guess what qualities of the man and what circumstances of his time account for his success and his failure (if indeed it was a failure).

John Lubbock was born in London in the middle of a significant period in our history, in 1834, just after the great Reform Act, just before the first Factory Act and the accession of Queen Victoria. His birth was in fact roughly synchronous with the birth of the Liberal party out of the tattered corpse of the Whigs. When he was very young the family moved to Down in Kent. His father was a baronet, a banker of very considerable fortune, a Fellow of the Royal Society and an eminent mathematician, the first since Newton to battle successfully with the difficult theory of tides. John has recorded his own first outstanding memories (about his third or fourth year) as a glimpse of Queen Victoria's coronation procession, and 'the sight of a large insect under glass'. This early interest in insects remained with him for life, but a much more important event occurred when he was eight. In his own words:

'I first heard his name in 1842, when I was just eight years old. My father returned one evening from the City, and said he had a great piece of good news for me. He excited my hopes and curiosity, and at last announced that Mr. Darwin was coining to live at Down. I confess I was disappointed. I thought at least he was going to give me a pony! But my father was right. I little realised what it meant to me, nor how it would alter my whole life.'

Darwin took to the small boy at once and very soon persuaded John's father to give him a microscope. So began a friendship which became only closer with the years till Darwin's death. It was firmly founded on both affection and respect, for, if the young Lubbock venerated Darwin, Darwin himself later confessed that he relied on the opinions of three men only, Hooker, T. H. Huxley and Lubbock: and of these he put Lubbock first because of 'the course of your studies and the clarity of your mind'; and Lubbock's introduction to scientific discipline was to report on some of Darwin's collections and to help in illustrating his work.

John went to a private school when he was eight and on to Eton at eleven. He was removed by his father before he was fifteen from motives which seem to have been mixed. Ostensibly and probably quite genuinely Sir John disapproved of the education given at Eton at that time, which consisted of Latin and Greek undiluted by science, mathematics, a modern language or even English, though history (ancient) and geography (classical) entered into it to a limited extent. But also, he had two ailing partners in the family bank and found that banking was getting in the way of his mathematics. Young John was made a partner forthwith: and with increasing frequency he was left to hold the fort while his father got on with the tides. So he had to face loneliness and responsibility very young: and, with a self-discipline almost incredible today, he set himself to remedy the defects of his education. He organized his day of 17 1/2 hours minutely, beginning with mathematics shown up to his father before breakfast and ending with German from eleven to midnight because, as he said, nothing else kept him awake so well. It is true that the time-table admitted three-quarters of an hour of whist after dinner and a walk in the afternoon as well as ample provision for prayer, meditation and the reading of sermons. Even so, it is hardly surprising that John's health was at this time thought to be uncertain. It is clear that he had already acquired the faculty of economizing time and of turning from one subject to another without pause or hesitancy which was the marvel of his contemporaries to the end of his life. As he grew up he became bearded in the fashion of the time, but it was probably policy rather than fashion which guided him in this: for, contrary to fashion and in the face of an indignant family, he insisted on wearing elastic-sided boots, remarking that one could easily learn a language in the time saved from doing up laces.

Space does not permit a <u>full</u> survey of his career, but an idea of his multifarious activities may be inferred from the outstanding events of three separate years in his life.

In 1856 (aged 22) he got married; he did the work on the reproduction of *Daphnia* which earned his admission to the Royal Society two years later; and he originated and secured the agreement of all other English banks to a major alteration in banking practice known as the Country Clearing System.

In 1871 (aged 37) within a year of entering Parliament as Liberal member for Maidstone, his first private bill became law as the Bank Holidays Act; his Ray Society Monograph on the Collembola and Thysanura was published (he first named the Collembola and distinguished them from the Thysanura); he became a Vice-President of the Royal Society and President of the Royal Anthropological Institute and was proposed as Vice-Chancellor of the University of London, an office which he held for the next eight years.

In 1888 he served on Royal Commissions on Elementary Education and on Gold and Silver, published what to a zoologist is probably his most important book: *On the senses, instincts and intelligence of animals,* became a Privy Councillor and President of the London Chamber of Commerce.

These three years have each an important zoological reference, but are not otherwise outstanding in the total of seventy-nine.

It is worth looking a little more closely at his parliamentary career. He was Liberal member for Maidstone for ten years and for the University of London for twenty before going to the Lords. He was never a minister and apparently never wanted office. His ambition before entering parliament is on record. It was:

1. To promote the study of science, both in secondary and primary schools.
2. To quicken the repayment of the National Debt.
3. To secure some additional holidays and shorten the hours of labour in shops.

In another place he admits that he was also at that time anxious to carry a measure to prevent the then rapid destruction of ancient monuments.

In the event he originated no fewer than thirty private member's bills which became law in his lifetime except for three which were still on the stocks at the time of his death. A considerable number of these are Acts regularizing the law as it affects commercial or professional practice, such as the Bankers Books Evidence Act, College of Surgeons Act, Dental Practitioners Act. The others are more directly related to what we should call 'raising the standard of living': and they show clearly how far Lubbock was in advance of his time: for example, The Open Spaces Act (1890); The Ancient Monuments Acts of 1882 and 1901; The Wild Birds Protection Act (1880); The Public Libraries Amendment Act (1892).

The way of the private legislator was even then beset by obstacles. It was only too easy for a meritorious bill to be thrown out or talked out for irrelevant reasons; and any serious opposition could block it for years. The Bank Holidays Act, Lubbock's first, got through at once on its tide, before opposing interests had time to mobilize. It was never intended as a measure for bank servants only, as its wording makes perfectly clear, but if it had been called a National Holidays Bill (which is what it was) it would certainly not have had so easy a passage. His second bill, on early closing, was, in fact, blocked in 1872 and finally got through in pieces after long delay as:

1. Shop Hours Regulation Act, 1880.
2. Seats for Shop Assistants Act, 1900.
3. Shop Hours Act (Early Closing), 1944.
4. Sunday Closing (Shops) Act, 1908.

In the early days there really was sweated labour in shops. Many never closed and the assistants slept under the counter when they got the chance. The first Act of the series only succeeded in limiting to 72 hours a week the work of young persons under 17. A twelve-hour day may seem to us more than enough for a child, but before the Act a seventeen-hour day was usual and even 120 hours a week not unknown. It took Lubbock thirty years of work to get an Act with teeth in it on to the Statute Book, but he was successful in the end. It is of interest that such important features of the Welfare State as holidays with pay and the forty-hour week stem from private motions of a Liberal more than fifty years before a Labour government was thought of.

His record of success as a back-bencher has almost certainly never been approached, and quite certainly never will be again. He stands alone. And the same qualities which made him successful there account for his successes in some other fields: he was known to be absolutely disinterested, and he was a born and also a highly-trained conciliator. If two eminent and pig-headed professors had been revelling for years in the sort of quarrel to which academic persons are prone, careless of whether they were wrecking every career and every enterprise within their ambit, Lubbock and Lubbock alone could persuade them that their interests were identical and that a common course of action was agreeable to both. And he could do this and still remain the friend of both. This talent became widely known when in 1871 he was called on to heal the breach between the Ethnological Society and the breakaway Anthropological Society. After that, the ambition of any society on the rocks through strife or incompetence, was to get Lubbock for President or Treasurer; and in fact he found time to be President of about twenty-five learned societies, ranging from the Historical to the Statistical, and about an equal number of commercial associations and government bodies. And he did work of the first importance in reconciliation during and after the industrial disputes towards the end of the century, especially the great Dock Strike.

The two great propagandists for evolution and natural selection were Darwin's personal friends, T. H. Huxley and Lubbock. And at first it seems odd that Lubbock, who was perhaps the more effective, should be less remembered. Huxley was a combative spirit who genuinely hated complacent ignorance in high places. His quarrel was not with the Church, but with churchmen who presumed to dogmatize without acquainting themselves with the facts. But he enjoyed the conflict, and if he could wipe the floor with a bishop or a canon of Christ Church it made his day; he does not seem to have been aware, perhaps he did not care, that though he usually silenced opposition he made few converts.

Lubbock took no part in these fireworks. As an evolutionist he believed firmly in progress and in human nature. He believed that if the facts were put to ordinary people in a way which neither insulted their intelligence nor twisted the knife in their deepest feelings, they were bound to reach the same conclusions that he had reached and to convince themselves of their truth. Experience showed that as usual he was right. He wrote books and they sold by the hundred thousand, edition after edition in every language under the sun.

His success is not really surprising, for he had hit on a technique then quite new and very rarely successfully copied since. He took the whole reading public into his confidence, and he never wrote down to it. There is hardly a book of his which could not be suitably read to the family before bed-time and which does not at the same time tell the expert much that he didn't know and suggest things he had never thought of. And he kept it up. From *Prehistoric times,* published in 1865, to *Marriage, totemism and religion,* in 1911, there is hardly a consecutive three-year period in which a book by him, important, influential and extremely popular, did not appear.

Books on botany, geology, archaeology, sociology and zoology; books on economics, and books on scenery, books on the pleasures of life and the history of coins: it seems incredible that books by one man on such varied subjects should always be readable and almost always of substantial scientific value, until one considers Lubbock's special advantages and abilities. He knew everybody who knew anything; he never forgot what he had heard or read or seen, and he kept to the end of his life the sense of wonder and the curiosity of childhood; he saw the relations between apparently unrelated things and he saw, with the clarity of the successful business man, the best thing to do next. He was the master of the wide view and the limited and attainable objective.

As an economist he originated no far-reaching and speculative theories, but he was one of the first to see that if economics was ever to be scientific (and he thought it might) it must have facts. It was his insistence on the publication of bankers' returns and every sort of commercial statistics, which has been instrumental in giving a later generation of economists the material on which to work. On coins and currency he could write not only as a collector (there were many collectors) but as a great archaeologist and as a banker who had sat both on Royal and on International Monetary Commissions.

He was not a great botanist, though he probably knew the flora of Europe as well as anyone of his time, but he could look at the plant world as an entomologist and an evolutionist, and he noticed that things which every botanist then took for granted needed explanation. His were among the first studies on form and function in plants, and he was the first to appreciate and to try to analyse the profound mutual influence of insects and flowering plants on their evolutionary histories.

As a zoologist, he wrote as one of the first to realize that it is what animals do that makes them interesting, and that the whole of classical taxonomy and anatomy and physiology is not an end in itself but an instrument for the understanding of their behaviour. He was also the first to appreciate that behaviour is only explicable in terms of the information animals receive from their environment. The order of the words in the title of the book I have already mentioned, is significant— *The senses, instincts and intelligence of animals.*

He was the first, after the great Reaumur, to realize the degree of intimacy necessary between an observer and the animal under observation before the latter's behaviour is susceptible of intelligible description. Even Reaumur could not keep ants alive and under observation for more than a few months. Lubbock invented the simple but satisfactory observation nest which is still standard, in which colonies could be kept under continuous observation for indefinite periods. He himself kept marked workers for seven years and had two queens of different genera which lived for thirteen and fourteen years respectively. He was the first to put identification marks on individual_insects, which seems an obvious thing to do now, like Columbus and the egg, but it gives him a claim to be the father not only of all sound subsequent work on the social insects, but of much of modern ornithology as well. He was the first to work out, with any degree of completeness, the extraordinary life-history of the domestic aphids which over-winter in ants' nests, and are literally put out to grass by the ants in the spring.

He was the first to use a maze as a device for the study of learning by animals, a method which has since been very extensively developed in the United States for testing the learning ability of vertebrates as well as invertebrates. He was the first to use the method of training which the Germans call `Dressur', as a test of sensory discrimination. This is the method which von Frisch has so successfully re-invented and exploited in the work of his school on the hearing and vision of fish, and the smell and vision of bees.

He first discovered that the path followed by ants depended, in certain circumstances, on the angle from which light was falling on them, and could be changed in direction quantitatively by moving the light source. This effect, rediscovered and christened the 'Lichtkompass Reflex' by Santschi (1911) forty years later, is basic to all subsequent studies of sun-navigation by insects and birds. And he refers, in parenthesis in his work on colour-vision, to an observation which anticipates the work of Hertz on form-vision in the thirties of this century.

The Peckhams, a pair of distinguished American entomologists, seem to have appreciated the importance of Lubbock's discovery of the light-compass reflex and accord him priority, but they make the singularly stupid reflection that it was a purely chance observation. If it was just chance, then it was just chance that Lubbock, on a walk before breakfast with Charles Kingsley, found the first fossil musk-ox to be recorded in Britain, and drew from this find the conclusion that the river gravel containing it was laid down in a glacial epoch. It was chance that led him on holiday in Switzerland to find an Eocene fossil in beds then supposed by Swiss geologists to be Triassic and unfossiliferous. It was chance that on the same holiday he found a parasitic wasp which uniquely uses its wings to swim under water.

It was chance that he should find, in the rubbish of his own garden, an animal which he called *Pauropus* — an animal then new to science and still of questionable status, though Lubbock's guess that it is a primitive sort of centipede is perhaps as good as any.

It was chance which enabled him to buy up Avebury, the finest megalithic monument in Europe, under the nose of the speculative builder who was proposing to wreck it, and to put a spoke in the wheel of the L.S.W.R. when they intended to build a branch line through Stonehenge.

It was chance that led him to Halstatt at the moment when the working of the salt-mines by the Austrian Government was beginning to expose the richest burials and cremations of the early Iron Age known in Europe. (It was, incidentally, Lubbock who first dearly distinguished the hunting

Paleolithic from the agricultural Neolithic cultures, and gave them these names which are still standard.)

If these were all chances, they were not the sort of chances which happen to ordinary people. But of course they were not chance at all. The animal which he named *Pauropus* had probably been seen by others and dismissed, if it was thought of at all, as the larva of something else. It was the natural thing to do, for zoologists had too frequently been caught out in giving generic or even family rank to larval forms of animals already well known as adults, and they were learning caution. But Lubbock had enough knowledge to be sure that there was nothing it could be the larva of, and enough curiosity to examine it carefully and show that it was sexually mature.

Only once does he seem to have been caught napping. Towards the end of his life he was invited with other distinguished persons to inspect the recently 'discovered' Piltdown skull, and he expressed a definite opinion about its age and importance. In his defence it must be said that he was old, he was ill and he was fooled in very good company.

How was it possible that such an extraordinary man should have been forgotten so completely? Some reasons can be confidently given. The first World War effected a far more complete break with the past than the last. In the twenties everything Edwardian and Victorian assumed a haze of unreality, even for those who were born before the turn of the century. Even to his contemporaries Lubbock had seemed a little incredible; to the post-war world he naturally appeared entirely fabulous. The class from which he came, the class of the fairly affluent whose sons had <u>filled</u> the professions and the public service as a matter of course, and which could afford to act from principle rather than for monetary advantage, was extinct: the men of military age were dead, and the women of necessity married elsewhere. For that class had predominantly provided 'officer material': and the half-life of junior commissioned officers in the 1914-18 war was only a few weeks. So government, local as well as central, passed into the hands either of the spivs who had done very nicely out of the war, or of people doubtless well-intentioned, but untrained and unprepared for that sort of responsibility. To neither did Lubbock seem to provide a satisfactory working model. He might truthfully have been described as an efficient idealist; and the Labour party, then as now, distrusted efficiency almost as much as the Tories distrusted idealism. He had been, if anything, a Liberal; and Lloyd George was busily engaged in the assassination of the Liberal party. He had been an internationalist; and President Wilson was sowing the dragon's teeth of 'legitimate national aspirations'. As a banker he was naturally suspect of underhand skulduggery; and if no skulduggery could be detected, that only showed how cunning he had been. As a scientist he was clearly the rankest of amateurs; and science was becoming more and more professional. No one, it was obvious, could possibly have done all the work which appeared in his name. There was something rotten somewhere. It was better to forget him, to depreciate him or to laugh at him.

And though no journalistic muck-raking has ever disclosed enough muck to make the smallest item of news, it is not difficult to laugh at Lubbock. Even his name is faintly comic. With unusual insight he had written home from school at the age of eight, telling his parents that he was quite popular because he did not mind being laughed at. It was true. Neither then nor later in life did he mind being laughed at, particularly if it served some cause he had at heart (though he was never so discourteous as to laugh at others unless he knew they were trying to be funny). He incurred a good deal of mirth among his contemporaries (including Ruskin) by giving in an address to a Working Men's College (and subsequently publishing) a list of the '100 Best Books'. Such behaviour seems to us both pompous and funny, especially in an eminent Victorian who had never been to a university, and could hardly be supposed to know. And to cite it became the stock method of disparagement. But Lubbock knew what he was about. He was very rarely mistaken in his judgment of the state of public opinion or in his recognition of a business opportunity, and he knew that if he gave his list enough publicity, someone would find it worth while to publish the books on it at a price the working man of those days could afford. And so it happened. Figuratively speaking, the last laugh was his.

So I do not think Lubbock can be said to have failed. Though he was human enough to enjoy the honours showered on him in his lifetime he never sought fame for himself, and would not have been distressed if it had passed him by. Of him, as much as of any man, it can be said: 'If you require a monument look about you.' The results of his life are unmistakably there, in science, in education, in the preservation of the countryside, in the less seamy aspects of the Welfare State; and if others now get the credit he would not have minded.

Perhaps the last word may be left to the late Aga Khan who, writing to congratulate him on his peerage, said: 'You have touched life at many points, done good service in many good causes and made wonderful use of your life and opportunities. Nor is it a light thing to have made no enemies.'

Printed in the United States
By Bookmasters